Paul Groves John Griffin Nigel Grimshaw

steps

A poetry course for GCSE

to Poetry

Contents

I know just how you feel

Look at it again

It's a shame!

Introduction

The poem on the page

You can recognise a poem as easily as you can recognise a dog. The most obvious thing about a poem is that it is set out in lines shorter than the ones you will find in a textbook or a novel. It isn't written in paragraphs, either, but it is often written in verses. For example, the sixth poem in this book, 'Visiting Miss Emily' has three lines to each verse.

There are other slightly less obvious recognition signals in a poem, too, such as rhyme or rhythm or metre. These are technical terms and there are many that apply to poetry. Technical terms, however, can get in the way of enjoying poetry. You can enjoy a poem without knowing any terms at all. Two or three are useful to know, however, because they can help you to a better understanding of the poem.

Rhythm

Heart beats, pop songs, walking footsteps have a rhythm. So does speech. This is because we stress certain parts of a word or certain words in a sentence. We say 'PHOtograph' but we change the stress when we say 'phoTOGrapher'. We say 'She TOOK a PHOtograph' and 'She MET a phoTOGrapher'. (The capital letters in those words and sentences show you how some parts of words or whole words are stressed, and some aren't.) These stresses give a rhythm to everything we say. When we read a poem, we either 'hear' these rhythms in our minds, if we read the poem to ourselves, or we actually hear them, if we read the poem aloud.

A poet can use these rhythms to make them 'echo' the meaning of the poem. Look at the poem, 'Stopping Places' on page 21. The rhythm of the first line sounds to us like this:

> The LONG CAR JOURneys to the SEA.

It is a slow rhythm. It 'echoes' the feel of a long, perhaps boring journey. The sixth line of the poem has this rhythm:

> viBRATing to the PASSage of FAST CARS.

which is a much faster rhythm – like the speeding cars. Some poems have a regular rhythm and there is another term for that.

Metre

Look at the poem 'Distracted the mother said to her boy' on page 28. The first verse has this regular rhythm.

> DisTRACted the MOTHer SAID to her BOY,
> 'Do you TRY to upSET and perPLEX and anNOY?
> Now GIVE me four REAsons and DON'T play the FOOL –
> Why you SHOULDn't get UP and be READy for SCHOOL'.

A regular rhythm like that is called *metre* and this bouncy, tumbling-along metre, repeated in the other verses, fits a clownish poem such as this. It might be argued that the use of regular metre like this gives a neatness and polish to a poem. The same could be said of the next term.

Rhyme

This is obvious enough. Some words at the end of lines sound the same. They rhyme: boy/annoy; fool/school. What isn't so well known is a short convenient way of putting this. Call the first word at the end of the first line 'a'. Call the word that rhymes with it 'a' too. Call the word that doesn't rhyme with either 'b'. Call the word that rhymes with that 'b' also. Then you can write out the rhyme scheme simply in letters. Look again at the verse printed above. Instead of saying that the rhyme scheme is one where the first two lines rhyme and then the next two and so on – which sounds a bit clumsy – you can say that the rhyme scheme is aabb.

Look at the poem called 'Oh, I wish I'd looked after me teeth' on page 62. The rhyme scheme of the first verse is aabba. Is it the same for all other verses?

Types of poem

Though you can recognise a poem easily, there are as many types of poems as there are types of dogs. They come in all sizes, shapes and characters. Many people think all poems are like poodles; they look pretty but they are only of interest to old ladies and children. But there are plenty of savage poems about, some very unpleasant ones; others are friendly and helpful; some are upsetting and disturbing.

Why write a poem?

If you read all the poems in this book, you will find that each one is about an event but it doesn't usually tell us a complete story. More often it is about a thought or a feeling. The poet wanted to share this with us, perhaps to convert us to a point of view, maybe to warn us, to annoy us, to make us cry or laugh, to show us something we had not thought of or to express in a fresh and interesting way something we *had* thought of. The writer decided that the best way of speaking to us was in poetry form. That way we might understand more sharply and clearly.

So there is nothing mysterious about a poem. A glance through this book will show you the variety of shapes and types of poem. The shape of the poem, the use of rhyme, rhythm, metre, the words chosen, the length of line and verses will vary with the subject and the aim of the poem. These differences, however, are important only in one way. How does the shape of the poem, the rhythm or rhyme and, most of all, the choice of words, help you to share what the poet felt and thought while writing the poem? Remember this when you are asked to write about poetry.

What to do with a poem

Read it. Listen to it. What does it make you think or feel? Read it again and discuss it with others. Or – try working in pairs. Each person reads a different poem and tells his or her partner what the poem is about. Then swap poems. Read them and see if you agree with the description given by your partner. Have you missed something that the other person noticed? Do you disagree about the poem?

Eventually you will choose some poems to write about. There is no single, fixed way to write about a poem but whatever method you use needs to be organised and systematic. Start by deciding what the poem is about. It is often best to work in pairs or small groups at this stage. Decide next what the purpose of the poem is, why the poet wrote it. Was it to show you something odd and interesting? To make you sad or to make you smile? Then look again. How has the writer conveyed the meaning of the poem to you? Look at words and phrases. Choose expressions of your own for what is being said. What is the difference between your words and the poet's? This process will help you to see the purpose of the poem more clearly.

Look at the sentence structure, the lines, the verse form, the rhymes, if there are any, the rhythm or metre. How does the choice of each of these help the meaning? How has the poem affected you? Do you agree with what has been said in it? Has it made you smile or feel sad or angry? Has it made you feel what the poet intended you to feel? Is there anything in your life that it has touched upon? If so, say why and how. Above all say what you really think, not what you think you are expected to think. 'I' should be a common word when you are writing about poetry.

The poems in this book

You will probably not like them all; we hope you like most of them. We're also sure you'll feel something positive about each one even if it's only annoyance. We've divided the poems into six sections to enable you to choose poems to compare and contrast more easily. Many of the poems have been chosen because of their unusual style; you can try different styles yourself. One good way of understanding how a poem is made is to pick one you like. Then try to write a poem of your own in a similar style.

Help

We are not going to tell you what to think or feel about the poems; you must decide that for yourself. After each poem, however, we have put down certain pointers. These are not to offer you a style or plan for your writing but, if you are asked to write an assessment or appreciation of the poem, we hope these pointers may give you some ideas. The pointers are set out as steps (see column opposite).

Use them as you like but remember they are based on our response to the poems. Each poem may set you off on a different track from ours and it is your own response and, we hope, your own enjoyment of these poems, that is important.

Step 1

Questions

Answering these should help you to make clear in your own mind some aspect of the poem.

Step 2

Statements

We have said what we think interesting about the poem. You may not agree. You may think some of our statements could be argued against. You may think they are just wrong – but they can be a basis for discussion.

Step 3

References

These are quotations. We have used them because we think they highlight an idea in the poem or are an interesting and exact use of words. Again, you may not agree. They are there for you to think about or talk about.

Step 4

Personal response

We have suggested something connected with the poem for you to write about.

Step 5

Section assignments

After the last poem in each section, there are suggestions for responses to groups of poems linked by the theme of the section. These are intended to encourage longer and more general pieces for folder assignments.

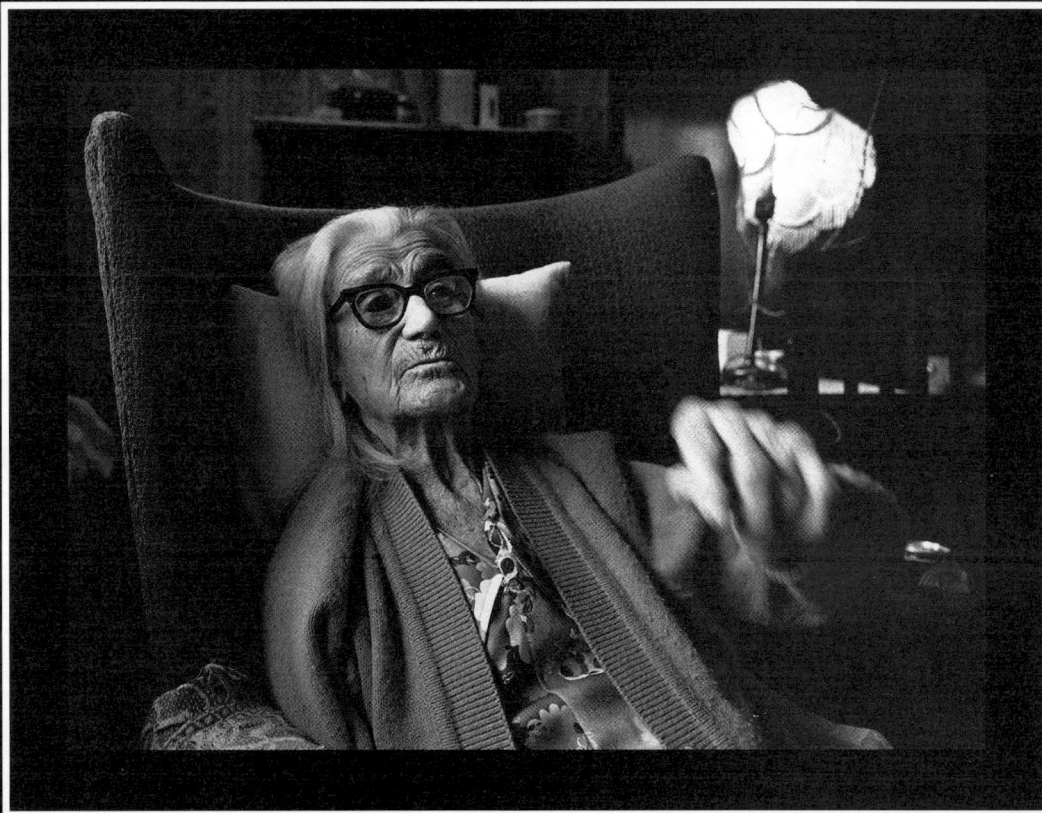

I'd never thought of it like that

The poems in this section are about people,
familiar sights or situations we think we know.
In each case the poet takes an inside or
sideways look, prompting the reader to re-think
and wonder: 'I'd never thought of it like that. Is
this true?'

POST OFFICE

E R

2

Collections

Monday to Friday

	0700
	1130
	1715

Saturday

| | 0700 |
| | 1200 |

Sunday   NIL
Good Friday   1300
Public Holidays NIL

Christmas Day and Boxing Day
NO COLLECTION

Uncle Edward's affliction

Uncle Edward was colour-blind;
We grew accustomed to the fact.
When he asked someone to hand him
The green book from the window-seat
And we observed its bright red cover
Either apathy or tact
Stifled comment. We passed it over.
Much later, I began to wonder
What a curious world he wandered in,
Down streets where pea-green pillar boxes
Grinned at a fire-engine as green;
How Uncle Edward's sky at dawn
And sunset flooded marshy green.
Did he ken John Peel with his coat so green
And Robin Hood in Lincoln red?
On country walks avoid being stung
By nettles hot as a witch's tongue?
What meals he savoured with his eyes:
Green strawberries and fresh red peas,
Green beef and greener burgundy.
All unscientific, so it seems:
His world was not at all like that,
So those who claim to know have said.
Yet, I believe, in war-smashed France
He must have crawled from neutral mud
To lie in pastures dark and red
And seen, appalled, on every blade
The rain of innocent green blood.

Vernon Scannell

Step 1

Questions

1 What is meant by 'Either apathy or tact/Stifled comment'?

2 Does the poem make Uncle Edward's affliction sound attractive?

Step 2

Statements

1 The poem tells us more about the author than about Uncle Edward's affliction.

2 The last five lines change the tone of the poem.

Step 3

References

'Grinned'

'savoured'

'His world was not at all like that,/So those who claim to know have said./Yet, I believe'

Step 4

Personal response

Add ten lines of your own, wondering about the world of Uncle Edward.

'All unscientific, so it seems': Find the medical definition of colour-blindness and its effects. Compare your findings with the imaginative version in the poem.

Suddenly, walking along the open road

Suddenly, walking along the open road I felt afraid.
I saw the stars and the world below my feet
Became a planet, and I was no longer
In Wiltshire, I was standing
Upon the surface, the edge of a planet
That runs around the sun.
I was in danger.
For all the comfort of the elms, the banal
Normality of houses with their garages, the apparent
Changelessness of the ploughed field on my right –
All was in danger.
A marble spinning through the universe
Wears on its dizzy crust, men, houses, trees
That circle through the cavernous aeons, and I was afraid.

Mervyn Peake

Step 1

Questions

1 What uncomfortable feeling does the poet have?

2 Why does he get this feeling walking at night?

Step 2

Statements

1 The poet is a very sensitive person.

2 He is walking through a familiar landscape gazing at the stars.

Step 3

References

'A marble spinning through the universe'

'dizzy crust'

'cavernous aeons'

Step 4

Personal response

How do you feel when walking alone at night looking into space: (a) in the town, (b) in the country?

What do you think of when you look up at the moon? Your thoughts may be very different to the poet's. For instance, this beginning might interest you: 'I just can't believe men walked on the moon. When I was small I nearly believed a cow jumped over it but . . .'

Following the cows through Ash

Following cows
through the village of Ash
on a bright October morning,
I see where the truth lies.

The massive, flat hips
like plateaux above cliffs
sway with the gradual earthquake
of their walk.

They are old women
who should wear black dresses
and black shawls, to go regularly
to mass, to mumble.

The sun is in front of them.
They are a deep forest against it,
dark thunderstorms of heavy flesh
against the light.

Their udders are weighted
with the labour of the cud
and the mansions of the chirping
cricket.

Walking in their wake, in cool
sun, clear as a miracle, the cowman
taps a hazel switch against his boot and
they know what this augurs.

The cows edge round a parked van.
One snuffles at the wheels and ambles
onward, ignorant in the rain-washed day
and the village street.

Then – one stops, turns its head,
watches me in my car. Its ears are up,
its eyes as placid as love. It has an idea
about me that I cannot touch.

Another, pausing to think again
its dream of nothing, tugs hard at lavender
bushing over stones: a twig, softly, shoves
its head aside. It lows.

And that is all. Cows. The sharp light
of the last of summer's dance. Their graceful
bulks. Nuts firming on the trees. Truth coming
easily as milk.

Martin Booth

Step 1

Questions

1 Does the poet like cows? What is the evidence for your answer?

2 What 'truth' does the poet understand from his encounter with the cows?

Step 2

Statements

1 The poet is held up in his car by a herd of cows. He does not get impatient but observes them closely.

2 Despite their clumsiness in the street he finds them to be graceful and loving animals.

Step 3

References

'. . . the gradual earthquake/of their walk'

'its eyes as placid as love'

Step 4

Personal response

Many people are afraid of cows. What is your response to them? In what ways are cows exploited by humans?

Write a close observation of a cat moving.

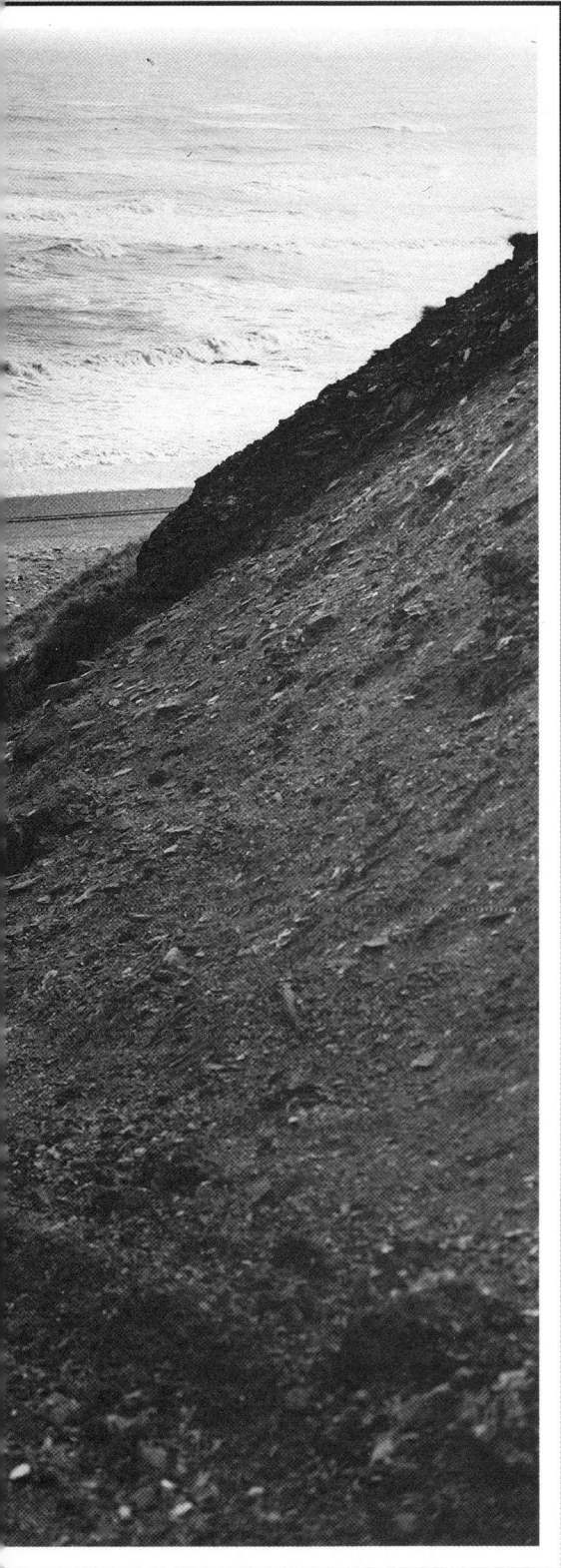

Sea coal

Thin square-shouldered men
scrape in the sea's wash
for coal,
hauling it out shining, seeming
still spongy: the beach runs blue
indigo.

Men long unemployed
and striking miners
fill bucket after bucket at the shallows,
arms and legs awash, glistening up to the joints;
trudge up the beach to the cart and the bored mare
grinding seagrass down between pale gums.

An east wind slashes in,
one man shivers, his bony shoulderblades
contract. The muscles work blue in his arms,
his shoes are crusted with sand and salt.

For one cold mile along the shore
ragged with dirty dunes, as far
as the power station breezing its cloud
of brilliant detergent,
the sea coal rises with the tide
far out, converges and comes in.

Pippa Little

Step 1

Questions

1 What is 'sea coal' and where does it come from?

2 Why can't the men simply buy their coal from a coal merchant?

Step 2

Statements

1 Gathering sea coal is a cold, hard, dirty job.

2 The poem, like a photograph, simply presents a picture.

Step 3

References

'. . .the beach runs blue/indigo'

'. . .the bored mare/grinding seagrass down between pale gums.'

Step 4

Personal response

What words and phrases in the poem suggest the cold and the fact that the men are poor?

Write, as if you were one of the sea coal gatherers, how you feel about the work.

Describe a scene, as the writer of this poem has done, where you or a group of people are doing a hard, unpleasant job of work.

Candles

The days of our future stand before us
like a row of little lighted candles
golden, warm and lively little candles.

The days gone by remain behind us,
a mournful line of burnt out candles;
the nearest ones are still smoking,
cold candles, melted and bent.

I do not want to look at them; their form saddens me,
and it saddens me to recall their first light.
I look ahead at my lighted candles.

I do not want to turn back, lest I see and shudder –
how quickly the sombre line lengthens,
how quickly the burnt-out candles multiply.

C.P. Cavafy
(translated by Rae Dalven)

Step 1

Questions

1 Why can the poet not relight the line of burnt out candles?

2 Why will he shudder if he turns back to look at them?

Step 2

Statements

1 The poem tells us how quickly life passes.

2 It is a poem of regret about the past.

Step 3

References

'golden, warm and lively little candles'

'how quickly the burnt-out candles multiply'

Step 4

Personal response

What sort of person, do you think, wrote this poem? A man or a woman? Was he or she old or young? What sort of personality did he or she have?

Do you think a line of candles is an interesting thing to compare the days of your life to? Say why. If you don't, suggest what you would use as a comparison.

Visiting Miss Emily

When you visit Aunt Em you must whistle
Through railings, and her face will glide
Like a white moon to the window-space

Then you must wait patiently
By the bruised door – (put your ear
Against it, you will hear how slow she comes).

When it opens, say with unusual breeziness
How are you then? But don't listen
For an answer. Instead, go down

Stairs murky as a lost century
And emerge in her underground cavern
Where a cat will panic in the darkness

There, make as much noise as you can –
Hum, whistle, scrape a chair – before
She enters with that curious and catching malady

Of never having been or done anything.
While you stay be on your guard.
She is a siren, although she weighs five stone

From some illness she has never recovered from,
Although her hair is thin and lank as a washing-up rag,
Although she keeps a finger crooked to stop a ring falling off.

Soon she will be capering for you, telling stories
Of how during the war she'd dive under the bed
So that the falling bombs would bounce back from the springs;

Of how the sole stripped from her shoe, and she walked
A mile sliding her foot to stop the cod's-mouth flap –
She flickers to life with visits; she forgets,

And soon you'll be groaning and wheezing, helpless.
But keep your wits about you; remember she
Is your kin. Haven't you seen somewhere

That paleness of eyes? That pallor of cheeks?
Haven't you known what it is to slump like that?
Isn't this cavern familiar? And the filtered daylight?

Wish her goodbye. Kiss her cheek as if it were lovely.
Thank her for the soft biscuits and the rancid butter.
Then straighten your tie, pull your cuffs square,

Think of tomorrow as a day when the real begins
With its time and teabreaks. Tell her you'll
Visit her again sometime, one quiet Sunday.

Brian Jones

Step 1

Questions

1 What things mentioned in the poem suggest that Emily is old and rather ill?

2 Does she get many visitors? How do you know?

Step 2

Statements

1 Though Emily is old and lonely she is still cheerful enough to make people laugh.

2 The writer of the poem wonders uneasily if his life will be like Emily's when he grows old.

Step 3

References

'By the bruised door – (put your ear/Against it, you will hear how slow she comes).'

'Soon she will be capering for you, telling stories'

'Think of tomorrow as a day when the real begins'

Step 4

Personal response

Do you find Aunt Emily a likeable character? A brave one? Or do you think she looks strange and it would be unpleasant to be with her? Give your opinion of her.

If you know an old person, write about what it is like to visit him or her, describing where he or she lives and what sort of food or drink you are offered when you go there.

Stopping places

The long car journeys to the sea
must have their breaks, not always
in towns where there's no room
to park but at the pavement's edge,
in villages, or by the woods, or in lay-bys
vibrating to the passage of fast cars.
The seat's pushed forward, the boot's lifted,
the greaseproof paper
rustles encouragingly. The children
climb to the ground and posture about,
talk, clamber on gates, eat noisily.
They're herded back, the journey
continues.
 What do you think
they'll remember most of that holiday?
the beach? the stately home?
the hot kerb of the promenade?
No. It will often be those nameless places
where they stopped, perhaps for no more
than minutes. The rank grass
and the dingy robin by the overflowing
bin for waste, the gravel ridged by
numerous wheels and the briared wood
that no one else had bothered
to explore, the long inviting field
down which there wasn't time
to go – these will stick in their memories
when beauty spots evaporate.
Was it worth the expense?
                              but
these are the rewards of travelling.
There must be an end in sight
for the transient stopping places
to be necessary, to be memorable.

Molly Holden

Step 1

Questions

1 What is necessary to make these stopping places memorable?

2 Why does the grease proof paper rustle 'encouragingly'?

Step 2

Statements

1 Sometimes you remember the stops on a holiday journey better than the holiday itself.

2 Things which you hadn't planned or expected sometimes stick firmly in your mind.

Step 3

References

'. . . It will often be those nameless places/where they stopped'

'. . . the long inviting field/down which there wasn't time/to go'

Step 4

Personal response

Do you remember stops on the way to a holiday? Do you agree with the poem? If so, has the poet mentioned the kind of objects and other things that stuck in your mind?

Write your own account, in prose or verse, of a long journey that you made. Include, if possible, details that had for you, a greater importance than you realized at the time.

Mrs Middleditch

Fitting a thin glove
Over a dry hand,
Over a gold ring (plain
As the nine-carat love
Of her good man now dead),
Mrs Middleditch pats
For the sake of tidiness
The back of her tidy head.

'It's time for shopping again.
I must think of the things I need,
Or *think* I need. Time
To go out. If I stay in
I mightn't go out at all.
I might give way to doubt
And ask, What *is* it all *for*?
And not go out of my door:

'And think, Why leave my bed
To wash and dress and eat,
And wash up, and wash out a dress,
And dress up, and go out for tea?
Sameness of fading days,
Is this what life should be?
Am I the slightest use?
And who will *ever* miss *me*?

'I must make out a list,
I suppose a widow must eat:
A caterpillar must eat –
But then, it can hope for wings.
Floor polish, cocoa, cake,
Sago, margarine, yeast –
A gruesome menu there
For my lonesome evening feast!'

'Oh, Mrs Middleditch, good
Morning to you!'
                'And to you!'
'A lovely morning again!'
'It is. (But you give me a pain;
What goes on in my head
You neither care nor guess;
One can have a little too much
Bright neighbourliness.)'

At the Supermarket door
An amplifier hails
Each housewife – and her purse –
With smooth false bonhomie.
Could anything be worse?
Mrs Middleditch hears
With a shiver of distaste
These words affront her ears:

'A Supermorning, madam,
For Supermarketing!
Our cut-price Superfoods
Are best for each and all
Our Supergoods await you
On every Supershelf,
So take a Superbasket
And help your Superself!'

'Oh, Mrs Middleditch,
This place is a boon!
I've come here for everything
Since my honeymoon.'
'Yes, yes, convenient,
Marvellous, I agree –
And yet I feel somehow as if
It's pressing in on me:

'There's too much of *everything*,
Too much advertisement,
I ask myself if what is said
Is ever what is meant –
FISH CAKES *taste breezy*,
CAKE FIX *bakes lightest*,
QUICK WAX *makes work easy*,
SQUELCH *whitens whites whitest*.'

'Oh, Mrs Middleditch,
Excuse me if I ask it.
But you've not got a single thing
So far in your Superbasket!
Let me recommend these peaches
And the nice thick double cream,
And you'll find the chicken breasts
(Milk-fed, of course) a dream.'

'I've got a list of things I need
Or thought I needed. Now I know
That peaches, chickens, cream,
And even sago, cocoa, yeast,
Are things I cannot buy today.
Today I fast, not feast.
I can't put out my hand, I find
A double vision in my mind.

'Beyond abundance – butter, eggs,
Strength-giving meat and cubes of cheese,
And cylinders of beans and peas
And syrup-swimming halves of pears –
Deserts I see, and frowsty rags,
And groups of persons wearing these,
Bowed by the weight of nothingness;
I recognize them – refugees.

'I see a child with seething flies
Fouling its big, unblinking eyes,
Eyes fixed on me: a swollen child
With dangling, thin, rachitic wrists,
Listless and silent, watching me,
In want and in unwantedness
Waiting to learn why it was born –
While I draw up my shopping lists.

'It will not do! I have no appetite
For food. And none for charity!
Dull, shiftless outcasts under static skies,
They are myself. Only the pelican
That tore her breast could teach me how
To reach that place, to staunch with work
That open sore, to feed with love
One orphan fed upon by flies.'

'Oh, Mrs Middleditch! Are you all right?'
Her answer was a sudden moan
And down she slumped upon the Superfloor,
The spotless floor of Non-Slip Superstone.
Inside her Superbasket was her head,
Unconscious prisoner of a Supercage.
'Quick, call the manager!' 'She was acting strange.'
'Silly old fool! she's reached the awkward age.'

William Plomer

Step 1

Questions

1 How do we know that Mrs Middleditch is in a depressive state of mind?

2 Why does she think of starving children in the supermarket?

Step 2

Statements

1 Mrs Middleditch is a prisoner in a cage of loneliness.

2 The poet finds the atmosphere of the supermarket a falsely cheerful one.

Step 3

References

'A caterpillar must eat – /But then, it can hope for wings.'

'A Supermorning, madam'

'There's too much of everything'

Step 4

Personal response

Write a letter about the plenty you see in the supermarket and the poverty of many people on this planet. It is for your local paper. You can suggest what people might do to help.

What should Mrs Middleditch do to fill her life with some interest? How would you advise her? You can reply as if you were an agony aunt, if you wish.

Emily writes such a good letter

Mabel was married last week
So now only Tom left

The doctor didn't like Arthur's cough
I have been in bed since Easter

A touch of the old trouble

I am downstairs today
As I write this
I can hear Arthur roaming overhead

He loves to roam
Thank heavens he has plenty of space to roam in

We have seven bedrooms
And an annexe

Which leaves a flat for the chauffeur and his wife

We have much to be thankful for

The new vicar came yesterday
People say he brings a breath of fresh air

He leaves me cold
I do not think he is a gentleman

Yes, I remember Maurice very well
Fancy getting married at his age
She must be a fool

You knew May had moved?
Since Edward died she has been much alone

It was cancer

No, I know nothing of Maud
I never wish to hear her name again
In my opinion Maud
Is an evil woman

Our char has left
And good riddance too
Wages are very high in Tonbridge

Write and tell me how you are, dear,
And the girls,
Phoebe and Rose
They must be a great comfort to you
Phoebe and Rose.

Stevie Smith

Step 1

Questions

1 Do you think the title is a suitable one for the poem? (Consider the type of material Emily writes, and the way the author means you to interpret the title.)

2 What might the author say to the charge that the poem's style was boring and disjointed?

Step 2

Statements

1 It's not surprising that Arthur 'loves to roam'.

2 There is a charity for 'distressed gentlefolk'. Emily should write to it.

Step 3

References

'So now only Tom left'

'*She* must be a fool'

'They must be a great comfort to you/Phoebe and Rose'

Step 4

Personal response

What kind of person is Emily? Young? Old? A person of many interests outside her family? Does she always tell the truth? Read the poem again and write down your impression of her.

The patricians

In small backyards old men's long underwear
Drips from sagging clothes lines . . .
The other stuff they take in bundles to the Bendix.

There chatty women slot their coins and joke
About the grey unmentionables absent.
The old men weaken in the steam and scratch at their
    rough chins.

Suppressing coughs and stiffnesses, they pedal bikes
On low gear slowly, in their faces
The effort to be upright, a dignity

That fits inside the smell of aromatic pipes.
Walking their dogs, the padded beats of pocket watches,
Muffled under ancient overcoats, silence their hearts.

They live watching each other die, passing each other
In their white scarves, too long known to talk,
Waiting for the inheritance of the oldest, a right to power.

The street's patricians, they are ignored.
Their anger proves something, their disenchantments
Settle round me like a cold fog.

They are the individualists of our time.
They know no fashions, copy nothing but their minds.
Long ago, they gave up looking in mirrors.

Dying in their sleep, they lie undiscovered.
The howling of their dogs brings the sniffing police,
Their middle-aged children from the new estates.

Douglas Dunn

Step 1

Questions

1 Pick three things that the poet says that are really observant about old men.

2 What things do old men wear?

Step 2

Statements

1 The poet understands the problems of old age from his observations in this street.

2 People suffer old age with dignity.

Step 3

References

'. . . their disenchantments/Settle round me like a cold fog.'

'Their middle-aged children from the new estates.'

Step 4

Personal response

How deeply does the poem make you feel about old age? How would you like to spend your latter years?

Write your own poem about an old person, being very observant about what you record.

Distracted the mother said to her boy

Distracted the mother said to her boy,
'Do you try to upset and perplex and annoy?
Now, give me four reasons – and don't play the fool –
Why you shouldn't get up and get ready for school.'

Her son replied slowly, 'Well, mother, you see,
I can't stand the teachers and they detest me;
And there isn't a boy or a girl in the place
That I like or, in turn, that delights in my face.'

'And I'll give you two reasons,' she said, 'why you ought
Get yourself off to school before you get caught;
Because, first, you are forty, and, next, you young fool,
It's your job to be there.
You're the head of the school.'

Gregory Harrison

Step 1

Questions

1 What signs are there, before the last line, that the poem is not meant to be taken seriously?

2 Why are the last two lines the shortest in the poem?

Step 2

Statements

1 The bouncy rhythm is suitable to the subject matter. The 'aabb' rhyme scheme helps the poem (the first two lines rhyme and the second two lines rhyme).

Step 3

References

'to her boy'

'you young fool'

Step 4

Personal response

Write the attendance officer's report on the skiving headmaster.

A removal from Terry Street

On a squeaking cart, they push the usual stuff,
A mattress, bed ends, cups, carpets, chairs,
Four paperback westerns. Two whistling youths
In surplus U.S. Army battle-jackets
Remove their sister's goods. Her husband
Follows, carrying on his shoulders the son
Whose mischief we are glad to see removed,
And pushing, of all things, a lawnmower.
There is no grass in Terry Street. The worms
Come up cracks in concrete yards in moonlight.
That man, I wish him well. I wish him grass.

Douglas Dunn

Step 1

Questions

1 How well off are the family who are moving and how do you know?

2 Why would the neighbours be glad to see that the little boy, the son, was moving?

Step 2

Statements

1 We can tell that Terry Street is a relatively poor area.

2 The poet hopes that the family are moving up in the world.

Step 3

References

'A mattress, bed ends, cups, carpets, chairs'

'. . . The worms/Come up cracks in concrete yards in moonlight.'

Step 4

Personal response

What kind of a person is the writer of the poem? Does he live in Terry Street? Is he old or young? Describe what you think he is like and how he feels about other people. Why, do you think, he wished the husband 'grass'?

Step 5

Section assignments

1 Choose two poems that, despite the title of this section, deal with thoughts, feelings, places or people that are familiar to you. Say in what ways the poet echoes your experiences. Give examples from your own life to illustrate your answers.

2 Choose two or three poems that deal with subjects that so far have been outside your experience of life. Say, for each, how well you think the poet has been able to make you share his or her feelings and make you more aware of the experience described.

Do you remember?

People like to look back, contrasting past and present. Other people's recollections can remind you of similar incidents in your own lives. Some situations you will be familiar with; others will be about times and places you will only have read about. You might conclude that though times change, people's feelings don't.

Our green house

Our green house
was where Beau Geste
ran
deep in the desert

Our gooseberry bushes
was where
I ambushed all the Wells Fargos

Our apple trees
was where
I played Tarzan
with my neighbour (Sally)
(She wasn't as pretty as Maureen O'Sullivan
but I forgave her when she rescued
me from hungry crocodiles)

The plum tree
was where
(it wasn't our plum tree but the branches
hung over the wall into our garden)
I boarded the Spanish ship
and saved the British Empire

Our pear tree
was where
I saved Sally from the giant

The pole
that kept the Monday washing up
was my
brother's own surrender flagpole
(Mum was angry when
he used my sister's knickers as a white flag)

The garage
without the car
was where
I judged the bad
and was judged when bad

The garage
with the car
was the plane
I bombed the Germans from
the ship I captained
the tanks I drove
the stagecoach I killed
Geronimo from
he died five times
(My brother said I was a lousy shot
the truth was that he was a bad loser)

The outside toilet
was the electric chair
(I didn't like that game
although I got to play James Cagney)

Our lane
was where I captained Ireland
against England at Rugby
kicked endless goals
was carried off the field
shoulder high
by my thousands of fans
and called the greatest ever
I won everything my heroes won
in our lane
I was the greatest ever
until I took a bath
then I was me again
the middle son in a family of eight
wearing my elder brothers'
hand-me-downs

Our house
was where
my mum and dad lived
and at night
it was the happiest place
I'd travelled all day

Richard Harris

Step 1

Questions

1 What kind of childhood did the poet have?

2 What advantages can you see from the poem of children having a garden to play in?

Step 2

Statements

1 The poet was much influenced by films as a young boy.

2 He had a very happy childhood despite wearing hand-me-downs.

Step 3

References

'The outside toilet/was an electric chair/(I didn't like that game'

'Our lane/was where I captained Ireland'

Step 4

Personal response

Make a list of your childhood heroes. In what way have these heroes influenced you? (Richard Harris became an actor.) Why might it be important to have heroes or heroines?

As a child, would you have enjoyed playing with Richard?

Describe one of the great feats you accomplished in your imagination, as a child.

Guy Fawkes

we wantud best Guy Fawkes
on ower street
so widressed ower lez
up
wipurra stick upiz back
a stick up each sleeve
one up each trahser
leg
an purrim in a barra

along Crown street
up Richo an dahn.
Big Barn Lane,
thed neva seen owt
like it
rait prahd wewus
weus pockets jinglin
an lez stiff as a
cork

wistopped ahtside this
misers ahhs an ah
knocked ont doower
'Penny fut guy mista!'
ah shahtud t'misruble
sod
an *ee* cum aht wavin
a big axe an ah
run

Lez cuddunt run cos
ee warrin barra
so wileft im
'ah'll geeya blewdy
guy' shahtud miser
an went t'chop it up

un lez jumped aht
fraitenin miser t'
death

miser dropt axe
anrun up path
an ower lez run
stiffleggud dahnt
lane shahtin 'Wayit
f'me! Wayit f'me!'

Barry Heath

Step 1

Questions

1 What is gained or lost by the poem being written in dialect?

2 What two pieces of evidence are there that Lez was a very convincing Guy?

Step 2

Statements

1 If you wrote the poem in prose it wouldn't make any difference to its impact. (Write out a verse in continuous prose before you make your judgment.)

2 The poet has made the whole thing up. It couldn't possibly be true. (Would it make any difference to your feelings about the poem, if it was totally true?)

Step 3

References

'Rait prahd', 't'misruble sod' – rait and misruble have two local meanings. What do they mean in the poem? Are there others? In what part of the country does the dialect and language show the poem is set?

Step 4

Personal response

Re-write the poem in your local dialect. Have you altered its impact or significance?

Write a poem about a childhood incident in your own dialect.

Write, in dialect, the conversation in which 'ower Lez' was persuaded to be the Guy.

Seasonal

As a young Londoner in Battersea
I had to calculate the time of year
by names and numbers, pocket-books of dates;
The Spring displayed few signals in the streets
though we bought sandals, shed overcoats.
Lavender Hill lacked blossoms, Queenstown Road
was loud with traffic, and grit-laden winds
blew all the year round, while, overhead
trains roared across reverberating bridges.
If any bird sang, every note was drowned,
and pigeons, nesting on high girder ledges,
must have been hatching squabs as deaf as stones.
Round Latchmere I remember sparrowlike
children, whose school was called the William Blake,
(who thanked his god he wasn't sent to school
to be transformed, by flogging, to a fool.)
The Latchmere kids had nowhere else to go
and came to school to play, during the evenings.
Some of them had no coats, and bare, chapped legs
were season-signs of winter.
I went by bus to work, down Queenstown Road,
between the park – a zoo of changing seasons –
and the Cathedral of Electric Power,
then over the opaque and fragrant Thames
to Chelsea where the shopwindows bloomed with dresses.
I told the seasons by their silly fashions.
I bought a black shirtwaister, with white stitches,
and a bright orange sundress, in King's Road:
then some voluminous, concealing smocks.
I should have guessed that blossomtime was over.
The sunset of the vernal equinox
fell like a redhot penny, through blue mist,
outside the window of the hospital,
near Clapham Common, where I bore my sons.
Now I look back across high Ribblesdale –
where I spent twenty years of changing seasons
and learned to read the date in roadside margins
and understand the festivals of birdsong
and tell the time by the inconstant clock
that's out of step with calendars: the Moon –
and from this Northern city I can see
that life in Battersea, through nine lost years
when I could never tell the time of year,

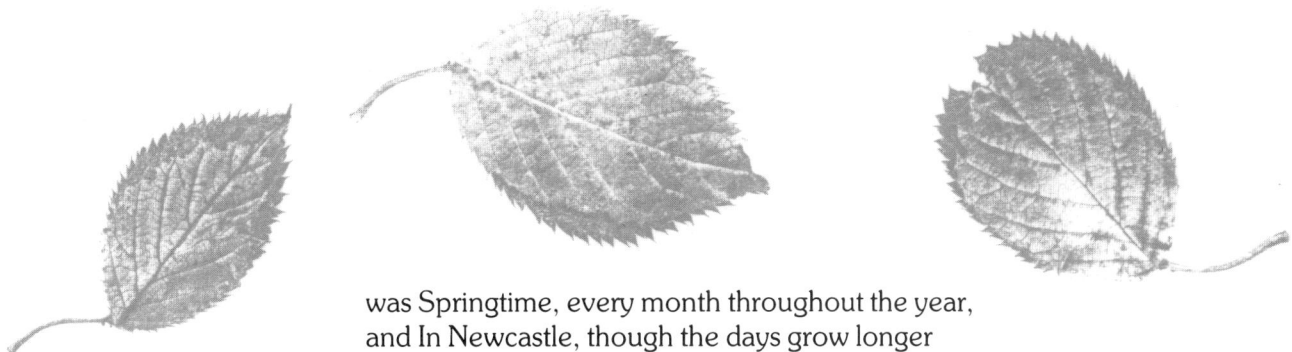

was Springtime, every month throughout the year,
and In Newcastle, though the days grow longer
and calendars say March, and buds say Green,
my season's Autumn and will soon be Winter.

Anna Adams

Step 1

Questions

1 How are the Latchmere children described?

2 How important is it to the poet to know what season it is?

Step 2

Statements

1 The poet contrasts the changing seasons in London and Ribblesdale (Northern countryside).

2 She looks back with some affection on the dirty, noisy urban landscape of London as she lives out her latter years in Newcastle.

Step 3

References

'trains roared across reverberating bridges'

'. . . shopwindows bloomed with dresses.'

'. . . learned to read the date in roadside margins'

Step 4

Personal response

How important to you is your environment? If you could change it what would you change it for? Is a town environment better for young than old people?

Another of those boring bomb stories, forty years later

I hope she didn't think I thought
that we was in the thick. I know we wasn't:
not like in Lewisham or central London;
we was just on the edges, at Burnt Oak.
I only said 'The smell of soot
brings back the bombing, when we was bombed out.'
Whenever I smell soot I think of that.
A Sunday afternoon, and Dad was shaving:
his Mum was coming on the bus from Hendon.
The tea was laid, and everything was ready
except for Dad in front of the small mirror
out in the kitchenette, all shaving lather.
Then suddenly, we was all of a heap
out in the hall, and the back windows broken,
and all Dad's shaving soap was black with soot,
and we was smothered: glass and soot and lather.
Whenever I smell soot I think of that.
It *was* a mess, but we was quite alright.
When we looked out we saw two houses missing.
Later we heard a man was crushed to death;
his roof fell in and he was underneath
the watertank. But then Dad's Mum arrived
and she was more upset than us.
There wasn't any tea. And after that
we lived in the front room. The back was open:
chickens came in and preened before the mirror.
Of course I know we wasn't in the thick;
I hope she didn't think I thought we was.

Anna Adams

Step 1

Questions

1 What happened when the bomb fell?

2 What did the teller not want the listener to think?
Why might this be?

Step 2

Statements

1 This poem is written in a conversational manner.
It could be two women talking over a cup of tea.

2 The poem is filled with details like the chickens
so we know it is true.

Step 3

References

'. . . Dad's shaving soap was black with soot'

'chickens came in and preened before the mirror.'

Step 4

Personal response

The poet says she wasn't in the 'thick' of the
bombing, as they were in Lewisham or Central
London. Write, as if you lived in one of those areas,
a piece beginning: 'They had it soft in Burnt Oak
compared to us!'

The Engine Drain

(a fenland memory)

It was the mighty Engine Drain, the Engine Drain, the Engine Drain,
Down which the water went, the water went, the mighty waters of the inland
   sea.
But still in memory I see, the inland sea
That did reflect the summer sky, when it was summer time, of
   Cambridgeshire.

The sky was blue, the sea was blue, the inland sea, the inland sea,
All blue and flat and blue and flat it lay for all to see.
The trees stood up, the reeds stood too, and were reflected in the mere.
As you might call that inland sea, you might have said it was a mere.
And in and out the branches all
The little birds did swoop and swing
Did swoop and swing and call
And oh it was a pretty thing to see them swoop and swing.
Oh ho the inland sea, the inland sea, the mighty mere that moved so prettily.

When winter came the water rose,
And rose and rose and rose and rose
And all about the cottage floors
It flowed and rose and flowed and rose
Till in their beds at night you'd see
Quite half afloat the midnight peasantry
That got their living hardily
And died of ripe old age rheumatically,
Oh it was quite surprising how
They'd live to ripe old age rheumatically.
It was because they early learnt
To put their boots on properly
Afloat in bed upon an inland sea.

And now I do remember how
Looking from shallow banks below
You'd see the little water-snakes
A-swimming to and fro,
So many little water-snakes
Careering round about
No man might stand to count them there
Careering in the pretty mere.

Oh it was merry in that day
To see the water-fowl play
Upon the inland sea,
Chip-chopping in the sea;
Or see them ride the water-race
In winter, till the winds in chase
Drove them ashore. Oh ho the wind upon the mere
It wound the waves in heaps and tossed the spray
That was half froze, upon the darkening day
Whipping the waters up till you might see
A mile away the whitecaps of the inland sea,
The whitecaps of the mere.

Ah me alas the day is past, is past and long ago
And no man living now might say he saw the waters flow,
All all are gone, the Engine Drain
Has took them to the cruel salt sea
And what is left behind?
A fertile flat and farming land,
A profitable farming land
Is what is left behind.
It took some time, as you might guess,
But not so long as you would guess,
A day or two, or two or three,
To take these waters to the sea
To take them to the Wash.

Why is it called the Engine Drain, the Engine Drain, the Engine Drain?
It was because the others were,
The other drains of Cambridgeshire,
Controlled by air, by windmills blowing there.
But oh this Engine was a force, a mighty engineering force,
It took the waters of the mere and brought them to the Wash,
It took them, did the Engine Drain, these waters of the inland sea
And droppt 'em in the cruel salt sea,
The cruel salt sea.

Stevie Smith

Step 1

Questions

1 Why is it a sad thing that the mere has been drained?

2 Why does the poet repeat words and phrases so much in the poem?

Step 2

Statements

1 The poem has a very haunting quality.

2 It reflects her deep feeling for the countryside and its people before it was tampered with by 'progress'.

Step 3

References

'The little birds did swoop and swing'

'And rose and rose and rose and rose'

'And droppt 'em in the cruel salt sea'

Step 4

Personal response

In what ways do you feel man has gone too far in tampering with the countryside? Have farmers shown a respect for the land and its wild life?

Imagine you are an historian. Write a paragraph, drawn from this poem, for a history book about the fenland.

The dare

Go on, I dare you,
come on down!

Was it *me* they called?
Pretend you haven't heard,
a voice commanded in my mind.
Walk past, walk fast
and don't look down,
don't look behind.

Come on, it's easy!

The banks were steep,
the water low
and flanked with oozing brown.
Easy? Walk fast
but don't look down.
Walk straight, walk on,
even risk their jeers
and run . . .

Never go near those dykes,
my mother said.
No need to tell me.
I'd seen stones sucked in
and covered without trace,
gulls slide to bobbing safety,
grasses drown as water rose.
No need to tell me
to avoid the place.

She ca-a-a-n't, she ca-a-a-n't!

Cowardy, cowardy custard!

There's no such word as 'can't',
my father said.
I slowed my pace.
The voices stopped,
waited as I wavered, grasping breath.
My mother's wrath? My father's scorn?
A watery death?

I hesitated then turned back,
forced myself to see the mud below.
After all, it was a dare . . .
There was no choice;
I had to go.

46   *Judith Nicholls*

Questions

1 Do you agree that the girl had 'no choice'?

2 Does the fact that she is a girl make any difference to your feelings about the dare?

Step 2

Statements

1 This is a dilemma that we have all faced in some form.

2 The girl's argument is not with the other children, her mother or her father. It is with herself.

Step 3

References

'Was it *me* they called?'

'a voice commanded'

'No need to tell me' (repeated)

Step 4

Personal response

Write a poem about a similar experience of your own. Use contradictory voices in your head in the same way the poet has done.

Janet waking

Beautifully Janet slept
Till it was deeply morning. She woke then
And thought about her dainty-feathered hen,
To see how it had kept.

One kiss she gave her mother.
Only a small one gave she to her daddy
Who would have kissed each curl of his shining
    baby;
No kiss at all for her brother.

"Old Chucky, old Chucky!" she cried,
Running across the world upon the grass
To Chucky's house, and listening. But alas,
Her Chucky had died.

It was a transmogrifying bee
Came droning down on Chucky's old bald head
And sat and put the poison. It scarcely bled,
But how exceedingly

And purply did the knot
Swell with the venom and communicate
Its rigour! Now the poor comb stood up straight
But Chucky did not.

So there was Janet
Kneeling on the wet grass, crying her brown hen
(Translated far beyond the daughters of men)
To rise and walk upon it.

And weeping fast as she had breath
Janet implored us, "Wake her from her sleep!"
And would not be instructed in how deep
Was the forgetful kingdom of death.

John Crowe Ransom

Step 1

Questions

1 Why is the poem called 'Janet waking'?

2 What effects has the poet achieved by varying
   the length of lines?

Step 2

Statements

1 The poem is an odd mixture of the comic and
   the serious.

2 It is not part of the poet's purpose to make you
   feel sorry for Janet or Chucky.

Step 3

References

 . . . Now the poor comb stood up straight/But
Chucky did not.'

'And would not be instructed'

Step 4

Personal response

Write about when you first realized ' . . . how
deep/Was the forgetful kingdom of death.' It might
take the form of a conversation between you and
one of your parents.

By St Thomas Water

By St Thomas Water
Where the river is thin
We look for a jam-jar
To catch the quick fish in
Through St Thomas Church-yard
Jessie and I ran
The day we took the jam-pot
Off the dead man.

On the scuffed tombstone
The grey flowers fell,
Cracked was the water,
Silent the shell.
The snake for an emblem
Swirled on the slab,
Across the beach of sky the sun
Crawled like a crab.

'If we walk,' said Jessie,
'Seven times round,
We shall hear a dead man
Speaking underground.'
Round the stone we danced, we sang,
Watched the sun drop,
Laid our hearts and listened
At the tomb-top.

Soft as the thunder
At the storm's start
I heard a voice as clear as blood,
Strong as the heart.
But what words were spoken
I can never say,
I shut my fingers round my head,
Drove them away.

'What are those letters, Jessie,
Cut so sharp and trim
All round this holy stone
With earth up to the brim?'
Jessie traced the letters
Black as coffin-lead.
'He is not dead but sleeping,'
Slowly she said.

I looked at Jessie,
Jessie looked at me,
And our eyes in wonder
Grew wide as the sea.
Past the green and bending stones
We fled hand in hand,
Silent through the tongues of grass
To the river strand.

By the creaking cypress
We moved as soft as smoke
For fear all the people
Underneath awoke.
Over all the sleepers
We darted light as snow
In case they opened up their eyes,
Called us from below.

Many a day has faltered
Into many a year
Since the dead awoke and spoke
And we would not hear.
Waiting in the cold grass
Under a crinkled bough,
Quiet stone, cautious stone,
What do you tell me now?

Charles Causley

49

Step 1

Questions

1 What does the last verse add to the poem?

2 What two things trigger the imaginations and fears of the children?

Step 2

Statements

1 The whole poem – what the children notice and think, even their purpose in the churchyard – successfully shows the innocence of childhood.

2 The poet adds to our understanding of the children's thoughts and actions by his use of similes.

Step 3

References

'Many a day has faltered'

'What do you tell me now?'

Step 4

Personal response

Describe an incident from childhood which ended when you ran away in fear.

When I was a kid

When I was a kid in Deptford
And financially insecure
I followed round the horse and carts
And shovelled up manure
Put it into sacks and sold it door to door
And at that time in Deptford
Of one thing I was sure
I would never make a fortune out of shovelling manure
Still the money I got came in handy
It paid for sweets and cinema seats
The *Wizard* and the *Dandy*
And everyone seemed happy
Including the milkman's horse
For without that noble creature's help
There'd be no trade, of course
So all the gardens blossomed
And all the birdies sung
And all the world rejoiced – because of horses' dung!

Dan Colman

Step 1

Questions

1 What does the poet really mean by 'financially insecure'?

2 Is horses' dung a subject for humour?

Step 2

Statements

1 This poem has a very happy feel to it.

2 The boy was actually doing something very useful in cleaning the street and helping the flowers to grow.

Step 3

References

'So all the gardens blossomed'

'And all the birdies sung'

Step 4

Personal response

How did you or how do you earn a bit of extra money? Is it better to earn money or be given it by parents?

Today we would say the boy was helping organic farming. What is your attitude to artificial fertilizers that pollute our rivers, etc.?

Write your own poem beginning: 'When I was a kid . . .'

Step 5

Section assignments

1 'Our vivid memories of childhood show just how important to us were those feelings and incidents that we later thought of as trivial.' Choose poems that describe incidents unimportant to adults and show how the poets have made them seem very important to children.

2 How do the poems in this section show that children remain the same from generation to generation?

I'm telling you

The poets in this section all have a different
point to make. They may choose to make it
solemnly or comically, but they all have
something definite to say to you.

The fat black woman goes shopping

Shopping in London winter
is a real drag for the fat black woman
going from store to store
in search of accommodating clothes
and de weather so cold

Look at the frozen thin mannequins
fixing her with grin
and de pretty face salesgals
Exchanging slimming glances
thinking she don't notice

Lord is aggravating

Nothing soft and bright and billowing
to flow like breezy sunlight
when she walking

The fat black woman curses in Swahili/Yoruba
and nation language under her breathing
all this journeying and journeying

The fat black woman could only conclude
that when it come to fashion
the choice is lean

   Nothing much beyond size 14

Grace Nicholls

54

Step 1

Questions

1 Why is shopping for clothes 'a real drag' for this woman?

2 How do the salesgirls irritate her?

Step 2

Statements

1 The woman is looking for clothes that are not tight fitting and will suit her figure.

2 There is a sense of her being in a cold foreign world.

Step 3

References

'Look at the frozen thin mannequins'

'to flow like breezy sunlight'

Step 4

Personal response

Write your own poem about the irritations of shopping.

Daniel Lambert

Daniel Lambert, a corpulent gentleman
Weighing upwards of fifty stone,
But nonetheless genial, athletic and polite
Was walking with his dog in Leicester
When he met a dancing bear.
The dog bit Bruin. Bruin's master
Beat the dog, and Mr Lambert
Hastened to rescue his pet.
In vain: the bear threw Mr Lambert down,
And there he lay, unable to regain his feet.
        Some people laughed (a fat man on his back
Is comical). But Mr Lambert bore it well,
He knew himself to be a personage,
Of normal size until the age of twenty,
After which he grew and grew
Into a figure, not of fun, but dignity.
His health was excellent, his strength
Proportionate to his appearance.
He shouldered hundredweights, bred hounds,
And fighting cocks, swam sturdily
In sea and lake, conversed with wit,
And won the hearts and high esteem
Of all who spoke with him.
Callers were welcome at his London home:
Price of admission, one shilling.
        He called himself the heaviest man
In England, supping water
While his bulk increased.

One evening in the year 1809
Nature rebelled against the trespass
She had borne so long. The clogged machinery
Of life stood still, this prodigy of mammon
Breathed his last, and on his couch
Lay numbered with the dead.
        His coffin, made of elm, stood on two axle-trees
And four clog-wheels. The church
Could not accommodate its width,
And eight men lugged it to a burial-ground.

The rest was briskly done:
The grave-yard gulped it down,
The sexton tucked the turf in place,
And worms began their surgery.
        Now he is liberated from the flesh,
His buoyant spirit races free.
Send your prayers coursing after Daniel Lambert's soul.
In heaven he's no weight at all.

Philip Oakes

Step 1

Questions

1 Was Daniel Lambert depressed by his great weight?

2 Apart from the date, what evidence is there that this is not about a modern day fat man?

Step 2

Statements

1 The poet has admiration for Daniel Lambert, historically Britain's fattest man.

2 He writes of Daniel Lambert's death as if it were a release from the prison of his body.

Step 3

References

'Price of admission, one shilling.'

'In heaven he's no weight at all.'

Step 4

Personal response

Write an account of an interview with Daniel Lambert, using details from the poem.

The O-filler

One noon in the library, I watched a man –
imagine! – filling in O's, a little, rumpled
nobody of a man, who licked his stub of pencil
and leaned over every O with a loving care,
shading it neatly, exactly to its edges
until the open pages
were pocked and dotted with solid O's, like towns
and capitals on a map. And yet, so peppered,
the book appeared inhabited and complete.

That whole afternoon, as the light outside softened
and the library groaned woodenly,
he worked and worked, his o-so-patient shading
descending like an eyelid over each open O
for page after page. Not once did he miss one,
or hover even a moment over an *a*
or an *e* or a *p* or a *g*. Only the O's –
oodles of O's, O's multitudinous, O's manifold,
O's italic and roman.
And what light on his crumpled face when he discovered –
as I supposed – odd words like *zoo* and *ooze*,
polo, oolong and *odontology*!

Think now. In that limitless library,
all around the steep-shelved walls, bulging in their bindings,
books stood, waiting. Heaven knows how many
he had so far filled, but still there remained
uncountable volumes of O-laden prose, and odes
with inflated capital O's (in the manner of Shelley),
O-bearing Bibles and biographies,
even whole sections devoted to O alone,
all his for the filling. Glory, glory, glory!
How utterly open and endless the world must have seemed to him,
how round and ample! Think of it. A pencil
was all he needed. Life was one wide O.

And why, at the end of things, should O's not be closed
as eyes are? I envied him, for in my place
across the table from him, had I accomplished
anything as firm as he had, or as fruitful!
What could I show? A handful of scrawled lines,
an afternoon yawned and wondered away,
and a growing realisation that in time
even my scribbled words would come
under his grubby thumb, and the blinds be drawn
on all my O's, with only this thought for comfort –
that when he comes to this poem, a proper joy
may amaze his wizened face and, o, a pure pleasure
make his meticulous pencil quiver.

Alistair Reid

Step 1

Questions

1 How thorough in his work is the O-filler?

2 Why might the library, knowing the O-filler was
   at work, have 'groaned woodenly'?

Step 2

Statements

1 It pleases and interests the poet to see the odd
   way in which the O-filler passes his time.

2 The poem includes a great many o's to give the
   O-filler pleasure when he comes to them.

Step 3

References

'. . . still there remained/uncountable volumes of
O-laden prose and odes'

'. . . Life was one wide O.'

'. . . and the blinds/be drawn/on all my O's'

Step 4

Personal response

What might a librarian have to say if he or she
caught the O-filler pencilling through the library
books? You could write the conversation in the
form of a play.

Write your own paragraph or poem to please
the O-filler. It should make sense but contain
as many o's as possible.

Warty bliggens the toad

i met a toad
the other day by the name
of warty bliggens
he was sitting under
a toadstool
feeling contented
he explained that when the cosmos
was created
that toadstool was especially
planned for his personal
shelter from sun and rain
thought out and prepared
for him

do not tell me
said warty bliggens
that there is not a purpose
in the universe
the thought is blasphemy
a little more
conversation revealed
that warty bliggens
considers himself to be
the centre of the said
universe
the earth exists
to grow toadstools for him
to sit under
the sun to give him light
by day and the moon
and wheeling constellations
to make beautiful
the night for the sake of
warty bliggens

to what act of yours
do you impute
this interest on the part
of the creator
of the universe
i asked him
why is it that you
are so greatly favoured

ask rather
said warty bliggens
what the universe
has done to deserve me
if i were a
human being i would
not laugh
too complacently
at poor warty bliggens
for similar
absurdities
have only too often
lodged in the crinkles
of the human cerebrum

Don Marquis

Step 1

Questions

1 Why does the poet choose a toad for his subject?

2 Why is 'warty bliggens' a suitable name?

Step 2

Statements

1 The poet means to surprise you into self-assessment at the end.

2 The language of warty is deliberately pompous.

Step 3

References

'do not tell me'

'ask rather'

'have only too often/lodged'

Step 4

Personal response

Write a poem in a similar style using an animal (a sheep, pig, snake or fox, for example) to make a point about human beings.

Oh, I wish I'd looked after me teeth

Oh, I wish I'd looked after me teeth,
   And spotted the perils beneath
All the toffees I chewed,
   And the sweet sticky food.
Oh, I wish I'd looked after me teeth.

I wish that I'd been much more willin'
   When I had more tooth there than fillin'
To pass up gobstoppers,
   From respect to me choppers,
And to buy something else with me shillin'.

When I think of the lollies I licked
   And the liquorice allsorts I picked,
Sherbet dabs, big and little,
   All that hard peanut brittle,
My conscience gets horribly pricked.

My mother, she told me no end,
   'If you've got a tooth, you got a friend.'
I was young then, and careless,
   My toothbrush was hairless,
I never had much time to spend.

Oh I showed them the toothpaste all right,
   I flashed it about late at night,
But up-and-down brushin'
   And pokin' and fussin'
Didn't seem worth the time – I could bite!

If I'd known I was paving the way
   To cavities, caps and decay,
The murder of fillin's,
   Injections and drillin's,
I'd have thrown all me sherbet away.

So I lay in the old dentist's chair,
   And I gaze up his nose in despair,
And his drill it do whine
   In these molars of mine.
'Two amalgam,' he'll say, 'for in there.'

How I laughed at my mother's false teeth,
   As they foamed in the waters beneath.
But now comes the reckonin'
   It's *me* they are beckonin'
Oh, I *wish* I'd looked after me teeth.

Pam Ayres

Step 1

Questions

1 What does the poet regret?

2 How does humour help to get her message across?

Step 2

Statements

1 This poem is written in the Oxfordshire accent and has a homely feel to it.

2 It would make a good advert for dental hygiene.

Step 3

References

'And I gaze up his nose in despair'

'As they foamed in the waters beneath'

Step 4

Personal response

Do you look after your teeth? Has this poem made you think about them? What other parts of the body can suffer through teenage neglect or behaviour?

Do you make jokes about false teeth? Write an advert for dental hygiene.

Write your own funny 'I wish I'd looked after' piece. The subject could be anything from your bike to your younger brother.

The song of the banana man

Touris', white man, wipin' his face,
Met me in Golden Grove market place.
He looked at m' ol' clothes brown wid stain,
An' soaked right through wid de Portlan' rain,
He cas' his eye, turn' up his nose,
He says, 'You're a beggar man, I suppose?'
He says, 'Boy, get some occupation,
Be of some value to your nation.'

I said, 'By God and dis big right han'
You mus' recognize a banana man.

'Up in de hills, where de streams are cool,
An' mullet an' janga swim in de pool,
I have ten acres of mountain side,
An' a dainty-foot donkey dat I ride,
Four Gros Michel, an' four Lacatan,
Some coconut trees, and some hills of yam,
An' I pasture on dat very same lan'
Five she-goats an' a big black ram,

'Dat, by God an' dis big right han'
Is de property of a banana man.

'I leave m' yard early-mornin' time
An' set m' foot to do mountain climb,
I ben' m' back to de hot-sun toil,
An' m' cutlass rings on de stony soil,
Ploughin' an' weedin', diggin' an' plantin',

Till Massa Sun drop back o'John Crow
    mountain,
Den home again in cool evenin' time,
Perhaps whistling dis likkle rhyme,

'Praise God an' m' big right han'
I will live an' die a banana man.

'Banana day is my special day,
I cut my stems an' I'm on m' way,
Load up de donkey, leave de lan'
Head down de hill to banana stan',
When de truck comes roun' I take a ride
All de way down to de harbour side –
Dat is de night, when you, touris' man,
Would change your place wid a banana man.

'Yes, by God, an' m' big right han'
I will live an' die a banana man.

'De bay is calm, an' de moon is bright
De hills look black for de sky is light,
Down at de dock is an English ship,
Restin' after her ocean trip,
While on de pier is a monstrous hustle,
Tallymen, carriers, all in a bustle,
Wid stems on deir heads in a long black snake
Some singin' de songs dat banana men make,

'Like, Praise God an' m' big right han'
I will live an' die a banana man.

'Den de payment comes, an' we have some fun,
Me, Zekiel, Breda and Duppy Son.
Down at de bar near United Wharf
We knock back a white rum, bus' a laugh,
Fill de empty bag for further toil
Wid saltfish, breadfruit, coconut oil.
Den head back home to m' yard to sleep,
A proper sleep dat is long an' deep.

'Yes, by God, an' m' big right han'
I will live an' die a banana man.

'So when you see dese ol' clothes brown wid stain,
An' soaked right through wid de Portlan' rain,
Don't cas' your eye nor turn your nose,
Don't judge a man by his patchy clothes,
I'm a strong man, a proud man, an' I'm free,
Free as dese mountains, free as dis sea,
I known myself, an' I know my ways,
An' will sing wid pride to de end o' my days

'Praise God an' m' big right han'
I will live an' die a banana man.'

Evan Jones

janga – a crayfish, found in some of the rivers of Jamaica.

'Gros Michel' (pronounced 'grow mee-shell') and
'Lacatan' are two varieties of bananas.

Step 1

Questions

1 In what part of the world does the banana man live?

2 What is a calypso and in what way is the poem like a calypso? Look at the rhythm of the verses.

Step 2

Statements

1 The banana man is delighted with his life and envies no one.

2 The poem praises the simple things of life like work, food, talk, sleep and nature.

Step 3

References

'An' a dainty-foot donkey dat I ride'

'Wid stems on deir heads in a long black snake'

'Praise God an' m' big right han''/I will live an' die a banana man.'

Step 4

Personal response

If the poem had not been written in dialect, would you have enjoyed it more or would you have enjoyed it less?

Imitating as closely as you can the rhythm of the poem, write your own verse about something you like doing. Your verse need not rhyme, if you find that difficult.

Teevee

In the house
of Mr and Mrs Spouse
he and she
would watch teevee
and never a word
between them spoken
until the day
the set was broken.

Then "How do you do?"
said he to she,
"I don't believe
that we've met yet.
Spouse is my name.
What's yours?" he asked.

"Why, mine's the same!"
said she to he,
"Do you suppose that we could be –?"

But the set came suddenly right about,
and so they never did find out.

Eve Merriam

Step 1

Questions

1 Why does the poet use 'Spouse' instead of a surname?

2 How do we know they do not communicate?

Step 2

Statements

1 You can often make a point effectively by wild exaggeration.

2 It has a nursery rhyme feel to it.

Step 3

References

'he to she'

'she to he'

Step 4

Personal response

The set breaks again. Continue their conversation in verse or prose.

Do you think television has killed the art of conversation?

Writing

and then i saw it
saw it all – all the mess
and blood and evrythink
and mam agenst the kichin dor
the flor all stiky
and the wall all wet
and red an dad besid the kichen draw
i saw it saw it all
and wrot it down an ever word of it is tru

You must take care to write in sentences,
Check your spellings and your paragraphs.
Is this finished? It is rather short.
Perhaps next time you will have more to say.

Jan Dean

Step 1

Questions

1 Is the writer making a point about the pupil or the teacher?

2 Why is the poem simply called 'Writing' rather than having a particular title?

Step 2

Statements

1 The teacher is conscientious.

2 The teacher has set ideas about what he or she is looking for.

Step 3

References

'Perhaps next time you will have more to say.'
(Would 'I hope not' be a reasonable response to this statement?)

Step 4

Personal response

Re-draft the pupil's writing accurately, and re-write the teacher's comments so that they praise the piece. Then say if your re-writing has in any way altered the point of the poem.

The early purges

I was six when I first saw kittens drown.
Dan Taggart pitched them, 'the scraggy wee shits',
Into a bucket; a frail metal sound,

Soft paws scraping like mad. But their tiny din
Was soon soused. They were slung on the snout
Of the pump and the water pumped in.

'Sure isn't it better for them now?' Dan said.
Like wet gloves they bobbed and shone till he sluiced
Them out on the dunghill, glossy and dead.

Suddenly frightened, for days I sadly hung
Round the yard, watching the three sogged remains
Turn mealy and crisp as old summer dung

Until I forgot them. But the fear came back
When Dan trapped big rats, snared rabbits, shot crows
Or, with a sickening tug, pulled old hens' necks.

Still, living displaces false sentiments
And now, when shrill pups are prodded to drown
I just shrug, 'Bloody pups'. It makes sense:

'Prevention of cruelty' talk cuts ice in town
Where they consider death unnatural,
But on well-run farms pests have to be kept down.

Seamus Heaney

Step 1

Questions

1 Why is the poem called 'The early purges'?

2 What is being purged?

Step 2

Statements

1 The poet has made the deaths of the kittens seem as horrible as he possibly can.

2 The poet has learnt to be like Dan Taggart.

Step 3

References

'tiny din' 'glossy and dead' 'as old summer dung'

'prodded to drown' 'false sentiments'

Step 4

Personal response

Recount a childhood fear that you have now abandoned.

Argue for or against the view that the poet's adult sentiments are the false ones. He, like Dan, has become brutalised by custom.

Stereotype

I'm a fullblooded
West Indian stereotype
See me straw hat?
Watch it good

I'm a fullblooded
West Indian stereotype
You ask
if I got riddum
in me blood
You going ask!
Man just beat de drum
and don't forget
to pour de rum

I'm a fullblooded
West Indian stereotype
You say
I suppose you can show
us the limbo, can't you?
How you know!
How you know!
You sure
you don't want me
sing you a calypso too
How about that

I'm a fullblooded
West Indian stereotype
You call me
happy-go-lucky
Yes that's me
dressing fancy
and chasing woman
if you think ah lie
bring yuh sister

I'm a fullblooded
West Indian stereotype
You wonder
where do you people
get such riddum
could it be the sunshine
My goodness
just listen to that steelband

Isn't there one thing
you forgot to ask
go on man ask ask
This native will answer anything
How about cricket?
I suppose you're good at it?
Hear this man
good at it!
Put de willow
in me hand
and watch me strike
de boundary

Yes I'm a fullblooded
West Indian stereotype

that's why I
graduated from Oxford University
with a degree
in anthropology

John Agard

Step 1

Questions

1 What is a stereotype?

2 In what ways does the poet jokingly suggest he is one?

Step 2

Statements

1 Behind the humour there is a feeling that the poet resents being regarded as a West Indian stereotype.

2 He is a highly educated man and has got his degree in a European culture.

Step 3

References

'I suppose you can show/us the limbo, can't you?'

'with a degree/in anthropology'

Step 4

Personal response

Do you tend to stereotype people from other cultures? How are people from your own culture stereotyped by people from other cultures?

Write a stereotype version of yourself – the behaviour and characteristics expected of a typical girl, boy or pupil.

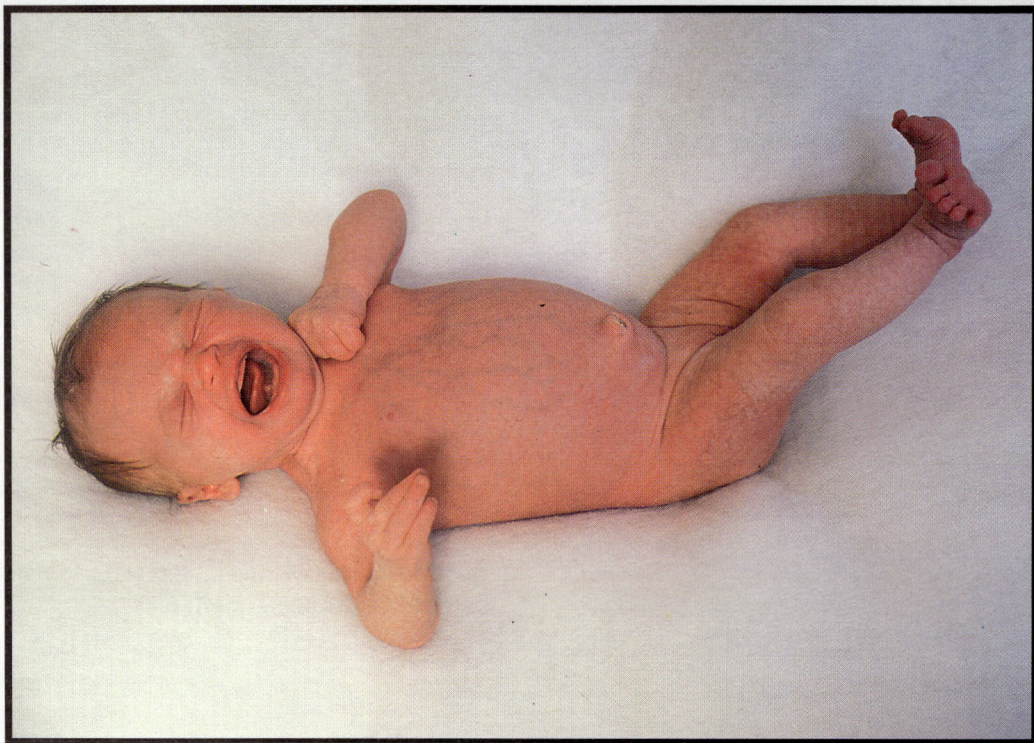

Baby song

From the private ease of Mother's womb
I fall into the lighted room.

Why don't they simply put me back
Where it is warm and wet and black?

But one thing follows from another
Things were different inside Mother.

Padded and jolly I would ride
The perfect comfort of her inside.

They tuck me in a rustling bed
– I lie there, raging, small and red.

I may sleep soon, I may forget,
But I won't forget that I regret.

A rain of blood poured round her womb,
But all time roars outside this room.

Thom Gunn

Step 1

Questions

1 What is the trauma of being born the poet writes about?

2 What does a person mean if he or she says 'I would like to go back to the womb'?

Step 2

Statements

1 The poem is about the shock of being born.

2 The baby rages because it has been plucked from comfort and security and shot into a harsh world.

Step 3

References

'But I won't forget that I regret.'

'But all time roars outside this room.'

Step 4

Personal response

Write a reply to this poem beginning:
'I don't want comfort and security.
The world may be harsh but it's exciting.'
(Say what you have enjoyed most about your life so far.)

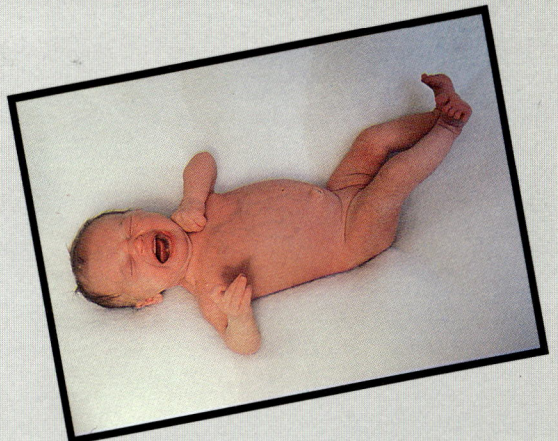

Step 5

Section assignments

1 Choose three poems in this section and, for
each one, summarise the message in one
sentence. For instance, 'Teevee' could be
summarised as follows: 'Families often show
more interest in television than they do in each
other.' Then show how each poet has made his
or her point more forcefully by writing a poem
than by using a straightforward statement.

2 Choose one serious and one funny poem and
show how the authors make their points in
different ways.

I know just how you feel

It is often comforting when you find your own thoughts and feelings reflected in others. The experiences described in these poems may be different from yours, but the feelings you have had in certain situations will probably be similar.

The old women

Go sad or sweet or riotous with beer
Past the old women gossiping by the hour,
They'll fix on you from every close and pier
An acid look to make your veins run sour.

"No help," they say, "his grandfather that's dead
Was troubled with the same dry throated curse
And many a night he made the ditch his bed.
This blood comes welling from the same cracked source."

On every kind of merriment they frown.
But I have known a grey-eyed, sober boy
Sail to the lobsters in a storm and drown.
Over his body dripping on the stones
Those same old hags would weave into their moans
An undersong of terrible holy joy.

George Mackay Brown

Step 1

Questions

1 Why would the grandfather when he was alive
   sometimes have to make 'the ditch his bed'?

2 Why might the old women, when they heard that
   the boy had been drowned, feel 'joy'?

Step 2

Statements

1 The old women dislike seeing anyone enjoying
   themselves.

2 They get a warped kind of pleasure from seeing
   tragedy overtake someone younger than
   themselves.

Step 3

References

'An acid look to make your veins run sour.'

'But I have known a grey-eyed, sober boy/Sail to
the lobsters in a storm and drown.'

'An undersong of terrible holy joy.'

Step 4

Personal response

Are these old women unusual in their attitude or
have you found some old people like them? Give
your opinion and illustrate it with some evidence
from your experience.

The diet

Sat in the pub
Drink flowing free
Everyone's merry
Cept poor old me
I'm starving

I have to sit
in the corner
All quiet
The trouble you see
I'm on a diet
I'm starving

No whisky, no gin
Why did I come in
no ploughman's lunch
like that greedy bunch
I'm starving

Shall I walk to the bar
I won't go too far
Just a pkt of crisps
and one drink
I'm starving

Then I think I'll have
when I've finished this fag
some chicken and chips
in a basket
I'm starving

No I can't keep quiet
I'll shout, Bugger the diet
I'm absolutely starving

Maureen Burge

Step 1

Questions

1 Is the writer weak-willed and silly to go into the pub where she faces temptation or do you sympathise with her? Explain why.

2 Does the slang and the swear word put you off the poem or does it add to the effect? What do you think of the occasional use of rhyme and the short lines?

Step 2

Statements

1 Because the writer is hungry, she is angry with the rest of the world.

2 Because she doesn't take herself too seriously, the poem is comic.

Step 3

References

'Everyone's merry/Cept poor old me'

'I'm starving'

Step 4

Personal response

Describe – or draw – an illustration to the poem featuring the person speaking. You will need to think about her size, the way she is dressed and the expression on her face as she looks at the others in the pub.

Hugger mugger

I'd sooner be
Jumped and thumped and dumped,

I'd sooner be
Slugged and mugged...than *hugged*...

And clobbered with a slobbering
Kiss by my Auntie Jean:

You know what I mean:

Whenever she comes to stay,
You know you're bound

To get one.
A quick
   short
   peck
   would
   be
   O.K.
But this is a
Whacking great
Smacking great
Wet one!

All whoosh and spit
And crunch and squeeze
And '*Dear* little boy!'
And 'Auntie's missed you!'
And 'Come to Auntie, she
Hasn't *kissed* you!'
Please don't do it, Auntie,
PLEASE!

Or if you've absolutely
Got to,

And nothing on *earth* can persuade you
Not to,

The trick
Is to make it
Quick,

You know what I mean?

For as things are,
I really would far,

Far sooner be
Jumped and thumped and dumped,

I'd sooner be
Slugged and mugged...than *hugged*...

And clobbered with a slobbering
Kiss by my Auntie

Jean!

Kit Wright

Step 1

Questions

1 How does the poet use varying lengths of line and different methods of emphasis to help give the feelings of the hug-mugged child?

2 How does the poet use repetition to emphasise the desperation of the child?

Step 2

Statements

1 The language conveys the child's feelings in a childish way. The strong verbs are the words that give the poem its force.

Step 3

References

'You know what I mean:'

'. . . bound to get one.'

'O.K.'

Step 4

Personal response

Write your own poem in a similar style about one of your pet hates or fears.

Dead men's shirts

Priscilla bought them at a jumble sale
'A bargain really and I knew you wouldn't care . . .'
Nor do I really, though can't help imagine
what was going on inside these stripes and creases
the last time they were worn.

Knowing what evicted their last tenants doesn't help
but my dear insists: 'That blue one had lung cancer,
this poor chap keeled over with a heart attack,
and that red check belonged to somebody who disappeared at sea,
they never found the corpse and rumour is he's done a bunk . . .'

I wear these other lives like armour,
know something of them by their taste in shirts
and there's a smell washed deep into the fabric that persists,
though no one else would notice it.

At first I would hear voices when I pulled them on,
fossil conversations buried in the weft,
could feel resistance to the routine of my dressing.
He buttoned from the bottom, always hung it on a peg,

whereas . . . I sense resentment sometimes, sometimes mirth,
as if the cloth were in a constant deja vu,
remembering how the Other one had spent like effort
to no particular end, had frittered time away
on things He knew were unimportant or mere sham . . .

I set to tame the shirts, impose my scent under the arms,
adjust the vents, take up a hem, sew name-tags along seams
establishing beyond all doubt that they belong to me.
But hung to dry a wind inflates the contours of their pasts,
reveals that other lives than mine still occupy their threads
our separate characters in conflict, now warping to adhere.

Stewart Brown

Step 1

Questions

1 How does the author feel in the fourth verse of the poem?

2 Explain what happens in the last verse when the shirts hang on the washing line.

Step 2

Statements

1 'Dead men's shirts' seems a very unlikely subject to write a poem about but the poet has made us think about wearing other people's clothes.

2 The poet writes about clothes as if they were almost living things.

Step 3

References

'I wear these other lives like armour,'

'fossil conversations buried in the weft,'

Step 4

Personal response

How do you feel about wearing other people's clothes from jumble sales, Oxfam, etc.? Write a poem about how you feel when you wear an item of clothing like someone you admire.

What do you find sad in this poem?

Long distance

Though my mother was already two years dead
Dad kept her slippers warming by the gas,
put hot water bottles her side of the bed
and still went to renew her transport pass.

You couldn't just drop in. You had to phone.
He'd put you off an hour to give him time
to clear away her things and look alone
as though his still raw love were such a crime.

He couldn't risk my blight of disbelief
though sure that very soon he'd hear her key
scrape in the rusted lock and end his grief.
He *knew* she'd just popped out to get the tea.

I believe life ends with death, and that is all.
You haven't both gone shopping; just the same,
in my new black leather phone book there's your name
and the disconnected number I still call.

Tony Harrison

Step 1

Questions

1 How do you know that both the writer's parents are dead?

2 Why did the father insist on being phoned beforehand by anyone who went to visit?

Step 2

Statements

1 The writer feels that his father's refusal to accept the mother's death was sad and pointless.

2 People who act unreasonably under strong emotion may know they are being unreasonable but go on acting in the same old way.

Step 3

References

'as though his still raw love were such a crime.'

'. . . the disconnected number I still call.'

Step 4

Personal response

The poem states facts rather than describing the writer's feelings. Write a paragraph saying in some detail what you think he is feeling.

Arthur

Everyone's got someone who gave them oranges,
Sovereigns or rubbed florins,
Who wore bottle-green blazers, smoked
A churchwarden pipe on St. Swithin's day,
And mulled their ale by dousing red-hot pokers
In quart jars.
But you, you're different.
You pushed off before the millions wrapped their puttees on
And ran away to sea, the prairies, New York
Where they threw you in jail when you told someone
Your blond hair made you a German spy.
After the telegram demanding
Your birth certificate
No one on the Island knew anything about you
Until the Armistice brought a letter
From a wife they'd never heard of.
You'd left her with the baby.
She wanted money.
You were somewhere in South America
In the greatest freedom, the freedom
Of nothing-was-ever-heard-of-him-since.

So I see you sometimes
Paddling up the Orinoco or the River Plate
With rifle, trusty mongrel and native mistress,
Passing cities of abandoned stucco
Draped with lianas and anacondas,
Passing their derelict opera houses
Where Caruso used to warble
Among a million bottles of imported bubbly.
Or else I watch you among the packing-case republics,
Drinking rum at the seafront in Buenos Aires
And waiting for your luck to change;
The warm sticky nights, the news from Europe,
Then the war criminals settling like bats

In the greasy darkness.
Your sister thought she saw your face once
In a crowd scene—
She went to the cinema for a week, watching
For your pale moment. She thinks
You're still alive, sitting back
On the veranda of your hacienda,
My lost great uncle, the blond
Indestructible dare-devil
Who was always playing truant and jumping
Off the harbour wall.

What I want to know is
How you did it.
How you threw off an inherited caution
Or just never knew it.
I think your grave is lost
In the mush of a tropical continent.
You are a memory that blipped out.
And though they named you from the king
Who's supposed to wake and come back
Some day,
I know that if you turned up on my doorstep,
An old sea dog with a worn leather belt
And a face I'd seen somewhere before,
You'd get no welcome.
I'd want you away.

Tom Paulin

Step 1

Questions

1 What relationship is Arthur to the writer?

2 In which part of the world does the writer imagine Arthur paddling up rivers?

Step 2

Statements

1 Arthur is an unusual person and lived a wild adventurous life.

2 The writer, imagining Arthur's probable adventures, finds him exciting to think about but would not like to meet him.

Step 3

References

'the freedom/Of nothing-was-ever-heard-of-him since'

'Then the war criminals settling like bats/In the greasy darkness'

Step 4

Personal response

Did Arthur have an exciting life such as the.one the writer imagines? Or did he have an ordinary life? Write your own ideas about what 'really' happened to Arthur.

Write your own poem about someone whose life you think was exciting.

The butcher

The butcher carves veal for two.
The cloudy, frail slices fall over his knife.

His face is hurt by the parting sinews
And he looks up with relief, laying it on the scales.

He is a rosy young man with white eyelashes
Like a bullock. He always serves me now.

I think he knows about my life. How we prefer
To eat in when it's cold. How someone

With a foreign accent can only cook veal.
He writes the price on the grease-proof packet

And hands it to me courteously. His smile
Is the official seal on my marriage.

Hugo Williams

Step 1

Questions

1 How might the butcher have come to know about the writer of the poem?

2 Why might the writer be a foreigner?

Step 2

Statements

1 The butcher is rather like the animals whose meat he sells.

2 The 'I' in the poem is a newcomer to the area.

Step 3

References

'His face is hurt by the parting sinews'

'I think he knows about my life.'

Step 4

Personal response

Write about how you were gradually accepted into a new community – when you changed schools, houses, or districts, for instance.

Home

After a summer's absence I return
in early darkness. The house, unlit

looks drear, extinct. My key scratches
in the lock and I enter half-surprised

by shrouded fustiness. Each room's familiar
yet strange with stored silence.

No room is living. Plants look queasy.
On the window sill lie flies and one big moth.

Yet at my coming life revives. I resurrect
the clock and listen to its gentle pulse,

sweep back the curtains and open windows wide
to sweeter air. The room breathes, relaxes.

But outside the garden crouches in the dark,
a wild thing, thirsting. Roses have bled.

I go out, a rain-god, sprinkling my largesse
to tame, reclaim. Soil hisses, yields

I hear its dank slow satisfying draught.
Going indoors, I feel the house becoming home.

William Cooke

Step 1

Questions

1 What does the poet feel about the house, which has been empty for some months, on his return?

2 Why might he put on the clock? Would it just be to tell the time?

Step 2

Statements

1 Poets write about smells as well as sights. You can smell the fustiness of the house as the poet describes it.

2 The garden is as important to him as the house.

Step 3

References

'On the window sill lie flies and one big moth.'

'I hear its dank slow satisfying draught.'

Step 4

Personal response

How do you feel coming back to your house or flat after you and your family have been away for a holiday? What you do first? How much do familiar home objects mean to you?

Grandma's funeral

There is nothing funny in a funeral, in principle,
Except the ritual, peculiar,
And one incident, particular.

    Bare trees, black and twiggy,
    Round the well-kept cemetery.
    Headstones in that desert
    Cramped our space around the hole.

The priest, some friends and relatives,
Not too surprised she'd died
At eighty-odd years old,
The reason for us meeting here today.

On the box, a crucifix played tricks
With us and with the moving clouds
For the last last time.
Pitter-patter scattering of soil on the lid,
Token of burial before the proper job began.
Sweaty work for someone, even in this hungry wind,
With such a pile to shovel in.
Then, my sister's turn; her cheeks burned...

    It was February. There'd been frost.
    The dainty lump she stooped to throw
    Was frozen, fixed to a bigger clump,
    And so, embarrassed, she launched the mass...

Down and down and downer still her send-off fell
As I tensed to hear the surely awful thud
From deep inside the solemn grave, the holy hole...
I heard it – boom! – like Grandma banging to get out.
"That'll wake the bugger up!" I said, aside.
Sister jabbed me as a substitute for sniggering,
Snorting down her nose.
Grandma would have laughed at that –
And at the gathering, sombre, still and sober,
When she had little time for any of those virtues.
There was warmth to spite a cold occasion.

Alan Barrett

Step 1

Questions

1 What shows the writer is not absorbed in the religious ritual, even before the incident?

2 How does the last line sum up the writer's feelings about the incident, the weather and the ceremony?

Step 2

Statements

1 There is a part of all of us that likes to see solemn occasions disrupted.

2 The humour is carefully used.

Step 3

References

'The dainty lump she stooped to throw/Was frozen, fixed to a bigger clump,/And so, embarrassed, she launched the mass...'

'...she had little time for any of those virtues.'

Step 4

Personal response

Write a conversation between two serious-minded relatives, giving a different slant to the incident.

Write a poem about your own embarrassing or funny experience at a solemn occasion.

Betrayal

As a mockery of late night treats
like trips to the fair,
that trip on the top of that tumbrel bus
to hospital
was worse, by a ninepenny fare,
than any wound
from any rusty nail.
"They won't prick me bum,
will they mum?"
Thoughts of young nurses,
mysteriously female and other:
girls using their craft
as a pass
giving crafty access to my bits and backside!

The hospital ward:
reassuring words from mum to son
of a jab – bad enough,
but a jab in the arm could be faced.
I was tough!
"Just wait in that booth there, please.
We'll be back in a moment or two."
We? Was she bringing her friends in to watch?
And why was mum smiling and nodding at her
as if she approved of all this?

On the couch, pants yanked down,
bare bum on display to the rest –
no time on an upside-down watch
for privacy or dignity
for just another someone-else's-kid.
Bared, I bore their bloody injection.
And I didn't cry.
I don't cry
when I'm angry
or betrayed.

Alan Barrett

Step 1

Questions

1 About what age is the boy? There are several clues. Why is the boy's approximate age important to the poem?

2 What use is made of the short lines in the poem?

Step 2

Statements

1 The poem is about adult conspiracy against the young.

2 Lies, however well intended, can always be harmful.

Step 3

References

'mysteriously female and other'

'giving crafty access'

'pants yanked down'

'on display'

Step 4

Personal response

Write the conversation between mum and the nurse.

Dumb insolence

I'm big for ten years old
Maybe that's why they get at me

Teachers, parents, cops
Always getting at me

When they get at me

I don't hit 'em
They can do you for that

I stick my hands in my pockets
And stare at them

And while I stare at them
I think about sick

They call it dumb insolence

They don't like it
But they can't do you for it
I've been done before
They say if I get done again
They'll put me in a home
So I do dumb insolence

Adrian Mitchell

Step 1

Questions

1 Why is the language so simple and colloquial?
2 What important word in the poem occurs seven times?

Step 2

Statements

1 The poem feels full of hate.
2 The poem gains from being written in the first person.

Step 3

References

'I'm big for ten years old'

'I think about sick'

Step 4

Personal response

Write a teacher's, parent's or cop's reply, in similar form, but with language more appropriate to an adult.

Step 5

Section assignments

1 The poems in this section are mostly about sad
  or irritating experiences. Write a contrasting
  piece, recalling a happy event that most people
  will probably have experienced at some time in
  their lives.

2 Choose the three poems that most closely
  reflect your own experiences. Describe the
  circumstances that made it possible for you to
  feel the same way as the poet.

The trap

The first night that the monster lurched
Out of the forest on all fours,
He saw its shadow in his dream
Circle the house, as though it searched
For one it loved or hated. Claws
On gravel and a rabbit's scream
Ripped the fabric of his dream.

Waking between dark and dawn
And sodden sheets, his reason quelled
The shadow and the nightmare sound.
The second night it crossed the lawn
A brute voice in the darkness yelled.
He struggled up, woke raving, found
His wall-flowers trampled to the ground.

When rook wings beckoned the shadows back
He took his rifle down, and stood
All night against the leaded glass.
The moon ticked round. He saw the black
Elm-skeletons in the doomsday wood,
The sailing and the falling stars
And red coals dropping between bars.

The third night such a putrid breath
Fouled, flared his nostrils, that he turned,
Turned, but could not lift, his head.
A coverlet as thick as death
Oppressed him: he crawled out: discerned
Across the door his watchdog, dead.
'Build a trap', the neighbours said.

All that day he built his trap
With metal jaws and a spring as thick
As the neck of a man. One touch
Triggered the hanging teeth: jump, snap,
And lightning guillotined the stick
Thrust in its throat. With gun and torch
He set his engine in the porch.

The fourth night in their beds appalled
His neighbours heard the hunting roar
Mount, mount to an exultant shriek.
At daybreak timidly they called
His name, climbed through the splintered door,
And found him sprawling in the wreck,
Naked, with a severed neck.

Jon Stallworthy

Step 1

Questions

1 Is the monster real or in the man's head only?

2 How has the author given the incident a nightmarish quality through both content and language?

Step 2

Statements

1 The title 'The trap' may have a secondary meaning.

2 The neighbours neither saw nor heard any evidence of the monster.

Step 3

References

'Ripped the fabric of his dream.'

'. . . his reason quelled/The shadow'

'. . . an exultant shriek.'

'. . . climbed through the splintered door,'

Step 4

Personal response

Write an account of the incident based on conversations with the neighbours.

At any rate

'He's dead!' they shouted as he left his motor-bike
And catapulted twenty feet through air
And dented earth. They wanted him to be dead
Out of a sort of innocent malignance
And being born dramatists the lot of them.
And dead he was in the end. The blood gushed
From his ears. 'He's dead,' they told the doctor,
Though he wasn't, as the doctor saw at once,
By any means dead. 'Officer,' they said, 'he's dead.
He ought to be at any rate if he's human.'
And in the end they were right, dead right.
An hour later, by the tangled bike
(Considered by the crowd by no means done for)
They were still standing, very much alive –
As they ought to be, at any rate if they're human.

James Michie

Step 1

Questions

1 Why did they want him to be dead? (Try to guess the meaning of 'malignance' before you check in a dictionary.)

2 Why does the crowd stay on after the cyclist is dead and, presumably, has been taken away?

Step 2

Statements

1 The poem is not about a particular crowd, it's about all of us.

2 The poet doesn't judge human behaviour; he simply describes it.

Step 3

References

'At any rate' (Note where the phrase occurs in the poem, and what follows it on both occasions.)

'very much alive'

Step 4

Personal response

Rewrite the poem beginning:

'He's alive,' they shouted as they reached the spot
We can see him moving underneath the lorry.'

Give your poem a 'happy ending', where the cyclist emerges unscathed after a seemingly dreadful accident. Then decide whether you have altered the point of the poem. Remember the crowd doesn't want death, just drama, whichever way it comes.

Finders keepers

This morning on the way to Charing Cross
I found a stiff upper lip
lying there on the train seat

Finders Keepers
I was tempted to scream

But something about that stiff upper lip
left me speechless

It looked so abandoned so unloved
like a frozen glove
nobody bothers to pick up

I could not bear to hand in
that stiff upper lip
to the Lost & Found

So I made a place for it
in the lining of my coat pocket

and I said
Come with me to the Third World

You go thaw off

John Agard

Step 1

Questions

1 What type of people possess stiff upper lips?

2 What is the Third World?

Step 2

Statements

1 The whole point of the poem is in the last line.

2 The poet could have made his point more effectively if he'd found the lip in a first-class carriage.

Step 3

References

'left me speechless'

'like a frozen glove'

'abandoned' (Why is the lip more likely to have been abandoned than lost?)

Step 4

Personal response

Write a paragraph describing how the lip became abandoned, something that induced its owner to change it for a quivering one.

The skip

I took my life and threw it on the skip,
Reckoning the next-door neighbours wouldn't mind
If my life hitched a lift to the council tip
With their dry rot and rubble. What you find

With skips is – the whole community joins in.
Old mattresses appear, doors kind of drift
Along with all that won't fit in the bin
And what the bin-men can't be fished to shift.

I threw away my life, and there it lay
And grew quite sodden. 'What a dreadful shame,'
Clucked some old bag and sucked her teeth: 'The way
The young these days. . .no values. . .me, I blame. . .'

But I blamed no one. Quality control
Had loused it up, and that was that. 'Nough said.
I couldn't stick at home. I took a stroll
And passed the skip, and left my life for dead.

Without my life, the beer was just as foul,
The landlord still as filthy as his wife,
The chicken in the basket was an owl,
And no one said: 'Ee, Jim-lad, whur's thee life?'

Well, I got back that night the worse for wear,
But still just capable of single vision;
Looked in the skip; my life – it wasn't there!
Some bugger'd nicked it – without my permission.

Okay, so I got angry and began
To shout, and woke the street. Okay! Okay!
And I was sick all down the neighbour's van.
And I disgraced myself on the par-kay.

And then. . .you know how if you've had a few
You'll wake at dawn, all healthy like sea breezes,
Raring to go, and thinking: 'Clever you!
You've got away with it,' And then, oh Jesus,

It hits you. Well, that morning just at six
I woke, got up and looked down at the skip.
There lay my life, still sodden, on the bricks;
There lay my poor old life, arse over tip.

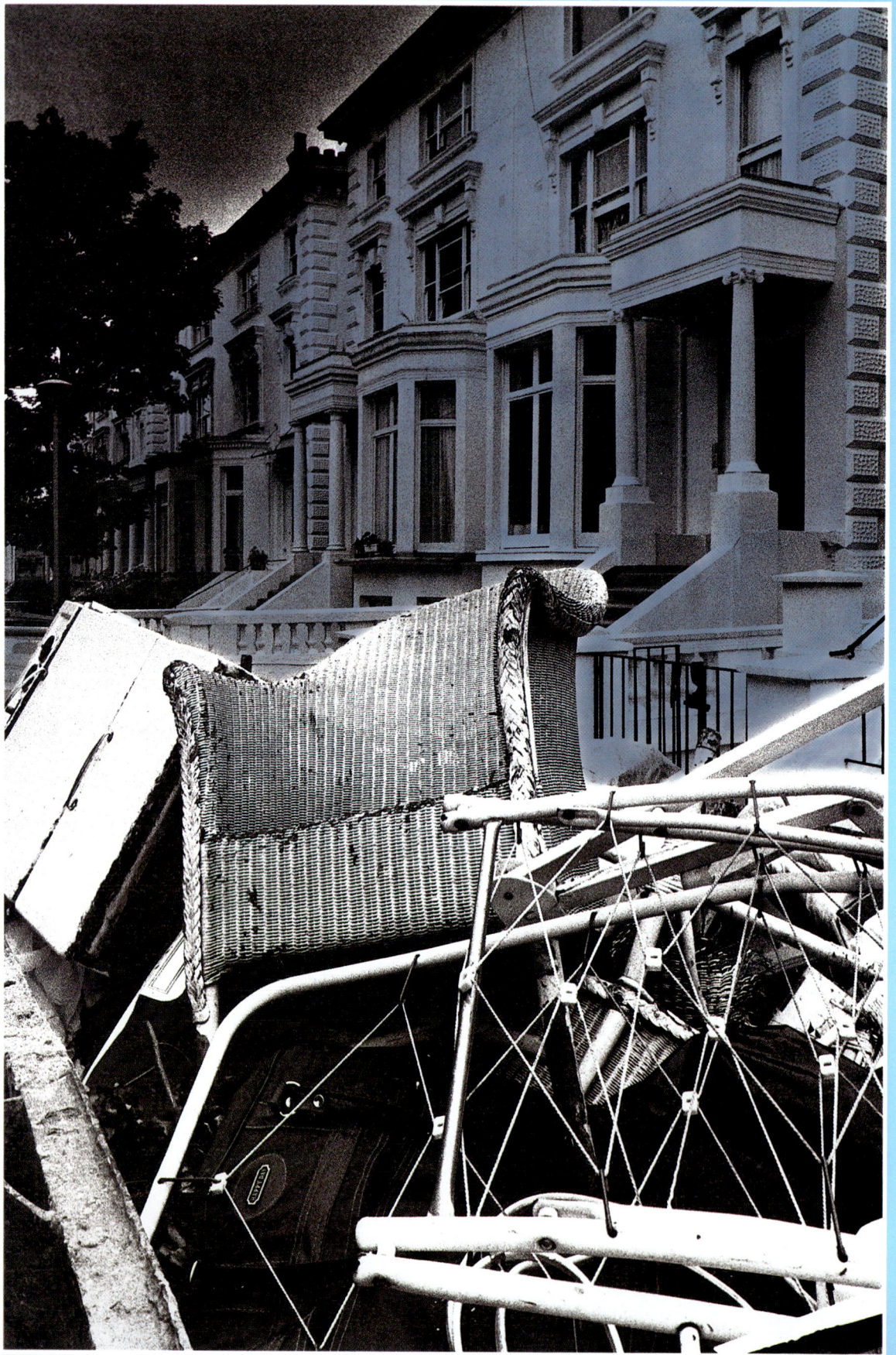

Or was it mine? Still dressed, I went downstairs
And took a long cool look. The truth was dawning.
Someone had just exchanged my life for theirs,
Poor fool, I thought – I should have left a warning.

Some bastard saw my life and thought it nicer
Than what he had. Yet what he'd had seemed fine.
He'd never caught his fingers in the slicer
The way I'd managed in that life of mine.

His life lay glistening in the rain, neglected,
Yet still a decent, an authentic life.
Some people I can think of, I reflected
Would take that thing as soon as you'd say knife.

It seemed a shame to miss a chance like that,
I brought the life in, dried it by the stove.
It looked so fetching, stretched out on the mat.
I tried it on. It fitted like a glove.

And now, when some local bat drops off the twig
And new folk take the house, and pull up floors
And knock down walls and hire some kind of big
Container (say, a skip) for their old doors,

I'll watch it like a hawk, and every day
I'll make at least – oh – half a dozen trips.
I've furnished an existence in that way.
You'd not believe the things you'd find in skips.

James Fenton

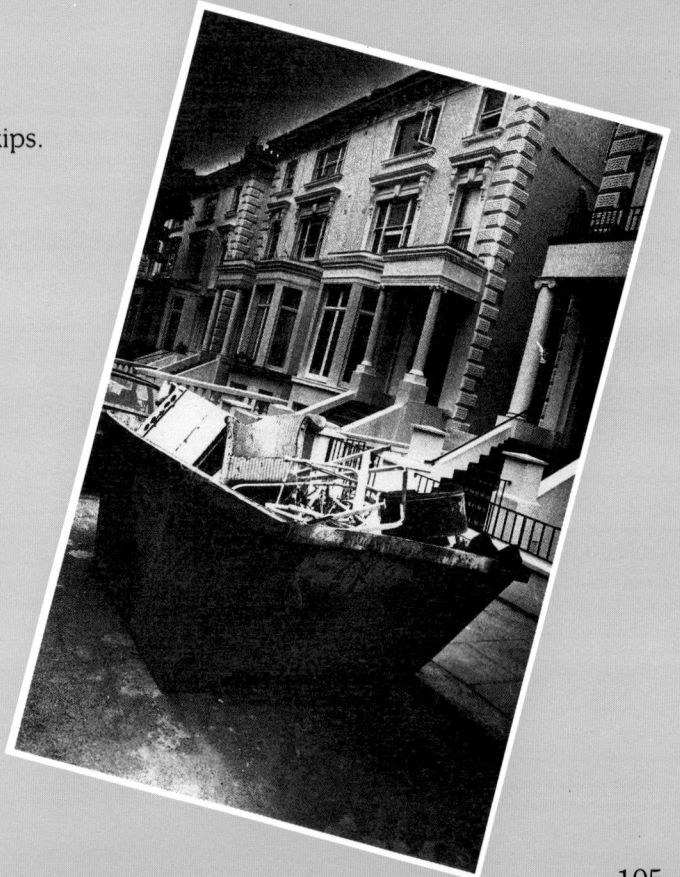

Step 1

Questions

1 What does the poet find after he throws his life away?

2 Why might somebody want to exchange their life for the poet's?

Step 2

Statements

1 This is an unreal poem – surrealistic you might call it. You cannot throw life away and still carry on living another life, yet the poem is full of truths about life.

2 The poem is saved from being maudlin, or indeed silly, by the poet's sense of humour.

Step 3

References

'Some bugger'd nicked it – without my permission.'

'You'd not believe the things you'd find in skips.'

Step 4

Personal response

How might the poet have got the idea for the poem?

What part of your life would you like to 'throw away in a skip'?

Defend this poem against the charge: 'I don't believe a word of it.'

The old couple

The old couple in the brand-new bungalow,
Drugged with the milk of municipal kindness,
Fumble their way to bed. Oldness at odds
With newness, they nag each other to show
Nothing is altered, despite the strangeness
Of being divorced in sleep by twin-beds,
Side by side like the Departed, above them
The grass-green of candlewick bedspreads.

In a dead neighbourhood, where it is rare
For hooligans to shout or dogs to bark,
A football in the quiet air is crisper
Than home-made bread; and the budgerigar
Bats an eyelid, as sensitive to disturbance
As a distant needle is to an earthquake
In the Great Deep, then balances in sleep.
It is silence keeps the old couple awake.

Too old for loving now, but not for love,
The old couple lie, several feet apart,
Their chesty breathing like a muted duet
On wind instruments, trying to think of
Things to hang on to, such as the tinkle
That a budgerigar makes when it shifts
Its feather weight from one leg to another,
The way, on windy nights, linoleum lifts.

F. Pratt Green

Step 1

Questions

1 Write some of the words and phrases that show that the old people have recently moved to a new home.

2 How do they feel about having moved?

Step 2

Statements

1 Even the budgerigar seems disturbed by the new surroundings.

2 The poem is about two old people lying uneasily awake, listening to faint sounds.

Step 3

References

'. . . they nag each other to show/Nothing is altered'

'It is silence keeps the old couple awake.'

Step 4

Personal response

Why have the old couple moved? (There is a suggestion about this in the poem.) What sort of neighbourhood have they come from? What do they think about as they lie awake?

Ferret

More vicious than stoat or weasel
Because caged, kept hungry, the ferrets
Were let out only for the kill:
An alternative to sulphur and nets.

Once one, badly mauled, hid
Behind a treacle barrel in the shed,
Throwing me back, Mathew slid
The door shut. From outside

The window, I watched. He stood
Holding an axe, with no gloves.
Then it sprang; and his sleeves
Were drenched in blood

Where the teeth had sunk. I hear
Its high-pitched squeal
The clamp of its neat steel
Jaws. And I still remember

How the axe flashed, severing
The ferret's head,
And how its body kept battering
The barrels, long after it was dead.

Stewart Conn

Step 1

Questions

1 Why had the ferret to be killed?

2 What happened after its head was cut off?

Step 2

Statements

1 Ferrets are small but very ferocious creatures.

2 The way they are kept and treated makes them more ferocious.

Step 3

References

'. . . He stood/Holding an axe, with no gloves.'

'. . . its neat steel/Jaws.'

Step 4

Personal response

Write your own poem about some real or imaginary scene of violence.

Explain, giving some examples, how the use of words, the punctuation and the way the lines break, help to give the impression of sudden, jerky violence.

Reading scheme

Here is Peter. Here is Jane. They like fun.
Jane has a big doll. Peter has a ball.
Look, Jane, look! Look at the dog! See him run!

Here is Mummy. She has baked a bun.
Here is the milkman. He has come to call.
Here is Peter. Here is Jane. They like fun.

Go Peter! Go Jane! Come, milkman, come!
The milkman likes Mummy. She likes them all.
Look, Jane, look! Look at the dog! See him run!

Here are the curtains. They shut out the sun.
Let us peep! On tiptoe Jane! You are small!
Here is Peter. Here is Jane. They like fun.

I hear a car, Jane. The milkman looks glum.
Here is Daddy in his car. Daddy is tall.
Look, Jane, look! Look at the dog! See him run!

Daddy looks very cross. Has he a gun?
Up milkman! Up milkman! Over the wall!
Here is Peter. Here is Jane. They like fun.
Look Jane, look! Look at the dog! See him run!

Wendy Cope

Step 1

Questions

1 How carefully has the poet followed the pattern
   of a real reading scheme? (The one you might
   have had in infant or primary school.) Is it
   important that she does so?

2 Should the poem be read in the same tone all
   the way through, or should the reading be more
   dramatic when the milkman enters?

Step 2

Statements

1 All the characters are stereotypes.

2 Contrast is the basis for the humour of the
   poem.

Step 3

References

'. . . She has baked a bun.'

'. . . Daddy is tall.'

'. . . You are small!'

'. . . in his car!'

Step 4

Personal response

Write your own reading scheme poem. Choose
any dramatic incident seen innocently through
childish eyes. Notice the poet hasn't overdone the
incident. It would have been less funny had
she been more explicit about the milkman and
Mummy.

Toads revisited*

Walking around in the park
Should feel better than work:
The lake, the sunshine,
The grass to lie on,

Blurred playground noises
Beyond black-stockinged nurses –
Not a bad place to be.
Yet it doesn't suit me,

Being one of the men
You meet of an afternoon:
Palsied old step-takers,
Hare-eyed clerks with the jitters,

Waxed-fleshed out-patients
Still vague from accidents,
And characters in long coats
Deep in the litter-baskets –

All dodging the toad work
By being stupid or weak.
Think of being them!
Hearing the hours chime,

Watching the bread delivered,
The sun by clouds covered,
The children going home;
Think of being them,

Turning over their failures
By some bed of lobelias.
Nowhere to go but indoors,
No friends but empty chairs –

No, give me my in-tray,
My loaf-haired secretary,
My shall-I-keep-the-call-in-Sir:
What else can I answer,

When the lights come on at four
At the end of another year?
Give me your arm, old toad;
Help me down Cemetery Road.

Philip Larkin

Step 1

Questions

1 Why does the last line of the second verse come as a surprise?

2 How does the poet give us the impression of work being a comforting old friend?

Step 2

Statements

1 The poet gives a vivid, but exaggerated, account of typical toad-work dodgers.

2 The poet suddenly uses striking colloquial phrases that contrast with the rest of the poem.

Step 3

References

'Hearing the hours chime.'

'Watching the bread delivered,'

'Turning over their failures'

Step 4

Personal response

Write about this comment on the poem:
'The poet only seems to prefer work because it is a more absorbing way of putting up with life. He makes both work and leisure seem unattractive.'

* Philip Larkin previously compared work to a toad that squatted on you, deadening your life. He wished to be rid of the toad work and live free to do as he wished. 'Toads revisited' shows how he has second thoughts.

111

Step 5

Section assignments

1 Use three poems from this section to answer the criticism: 'Poetry has nothing to do with ordinary life.'

2 'The people behind the poems'. Use this title to describe what you imagine two of the poets in this section would be like if you met them. Refer to their poems to support your answer.

It's a shame!

What goes into chicken pies

(in memory of Alan Bell)

Shortly before he died he rang
to tell me everything was fine – he'd got this job
cutting chickens up for pies. Well, it was something.
The pay was bad, the hours long, after work
he just felt like sleeping, nothing else –
but it was something. He liked the people, they were
looking after him, he said. He kept apologizing
for taking up my time, but everything was fine –
only, he'd cut his hand again.

When I remember how he died I see him on the early shift,
the blade much sharper, more awake than he is,
flicking between his sleepy fingers – I see him
fumbling hour after hour to reach his quota, tray after tray
of bald, colourless, featureless birds,
stunned, scalded and boiled for the blade,
the battery hens, the conveyor belts, the early shift,
the hot meat slipping from pink fingers. It wasn't
the overdose that killed him but the cut
that would not heal, that all his life had bled

failure at home and school,
childhood poverty and adult loss,
rooms that never dried, streets never swept,
lousy food and endless colds and pains,
hospitals and mental homes, shock-treatment in his teens
that knackered his brain and left him only
convinced he was stupid, depression, the darkened rooms,
the dying father, the broken marriage, the worthlessness
of the daily grind, ceaseless worry wearing him down,
wearing him out year after valium-laden year,
the children too far away to visit, too far away,
the damp carpets, unpainted sills, unweeded garden, the cat
trapped on the wrong side of the door, the despair
of simply being allowed to dream, the sleepless,
half-drugged solitude, the restlessness.

No overdose, however large, could heal that lifelong cut.
He just rang to tell me everything was fine
and warn me what goes into chicken pies.

Cal Clothier

Step 1

Questions

1 What two things does the writer say killed the man who died?

2 Was his death an accident or not? Say why you think so.

Step 2

Statements

1 The man's death is sadder because he did not complain about his life.

2 What goes into chicken pies is the lives of the people who make them.

Step 3

References

'wearing him out year after valium-laden year'

'No overdose, however large, could heal that lifelong cut.'

Step 4

Personal response

How old was the man who died? Where did he live? Describe what you think he looked like and the place where he lived.

Huntsman blow your bloody horn

Huntsman, blow your bloody horn;
Drink the wine and make a start;
Noble men on noble horses,
Gone to tear a fox apart.

I touch my forelock for my betters;
Huntsman, blow your silver horn;
Noble men on noble horses
Hunt bold Reynard in the morn.
Hunt to help the local farmer,
Keep bold Reynard from his door.
Foxhunting is so efficient;
That sometimes we breed some more.
Huntsman, blow your bloody horn;
Drink the wine and make a start;
Noble men on noble horses,
Gone to tear a fox apart.
Shed no tears for bold old Reynard:
Noble Reynard loves the chase,
To face the noble teeth of foxhounds;
Torn to bits but not disgraced.
Noble Reynard loves the hunt, Sir;
Use the whip, sir, use the spur;
Catch the end of happy Reynard,
Laughing in the blood and fur.
Huntsman, blow your bloody horn,
Drink the wine and make a start;
Noble men on noble horses,
Gone to tear a fox apart.

Horseman, riding over hedges,
With your cry of, 'view halloo',
Would you cherish final vict'ry
If such death would come to you?
If foxhounds tore you limb from limb, Sir,
Would you find it noble then?
Would you meet a happy death, Sir,
Making sport for gentlemen?
Huntsman blow your bloody horn;
Drink the wine and make a start;
Noble men on noble horses,
Gone to tear a fox apart.

Les Barker

Step 1

Questions

1 Why does the poet use the word 'noble' so much?

2 What is the effect of ending each verse with the same lines?

Step 2

Statements

1 This poem is written in a sarcastic way.

2 The metre has the urgency of the gallop of the chase in it.

Step 3

References

'Hunstman, blow your bloody horn;'

'Catch the end of happy Reynard,'

Step 4

Personal response

What is your reaction to this poem? Is it overdone? Could it have been said more simply? How can a poem help a cause?

Ballad of the two left hands

When walking out one morning
    Walking down Clydeside Street
I met a man with two left hands
    Who said he was obsolete.

At noon the work horns sounded through
    The shipyards on Clyde's shore
And told men that the day had come
    When they'd work there no more.

Economy is hand and sweat
    A welder in his mask
A new apprentice pouring tea
    From his father's thermos flask.

And soon these men of several trades
    Stood there on Clydeside Street
Stood staring at each new left hand
    That made them obsolete.

'Beware of men in suits,' one said
    'Take it from me, it's true
Their drivel economics'll
    Put two left hands on you.'

All in the afternoon was shut
    When I walked out again
The day had pulled on its black gloves
    And turned its back on men.

I walked the dusk of darkened cranes
    Clyde broke on Clyde's dark shore
And rivets fired where men still work
    Though men work here no more.

High in the night's dark universe
    I saw the promised star
That men I knew raise glasses to
    In an illegal bar.

They toast the city still to come
    Where truth and justice meet
And though they don't know where it is
    It's not on Clydeside Street.

With thumbs stuck on the wrong way round
    In two left-footed shoes
I saw a man search in his heart
    And ask it, 'Are you true?'

The man who sat in Clydeside Street
    Looked up at me and said
'I'll study this, then I'll pick clean
    The insides of my head.'

And moonlight washed the shipyards then
    Each crane was hung with stars
Rinsed in the moonlight we stared up
    Like old astronomers.

Economy is hand and sweat
    And foundrymen and fire
Revise your textbooks, multiply
    Your guilt by your desire.

Such dignity, so many lives,
    Even on Clydeside Street
When mind and heart together ask
    'Why are we obsolete?'

Douglas Dunn

Step 1

Questions

1 Why is the poem called 'Ballad of the two left hands?

2 Quote some lines showing the despair of unemployment.

Step 2

Statements

1 The poet has great empathy with men put out of work through no fault of their own.

2 The ballad form makes this a haunting poem.

Step 3

References

'Beware of men in suits'

'The day has pulled on its black gloves'

'With thumbs stuck on the wrong way round'

Step 4

Personal response

How has the poet made you sympathise with the men who are obsolete?

Miss Williams and the death-watch beetle

The death-watch beetle from the church
Got into Miss Williams' head;
Flew from the church timbers
And lived in her brain instead.

Tick, tick, tick went the beetle,
At night it was very bad,
But even in the day time
It drove Miss Williams mad.

And her pale blue eyes were haunted
With the overwhelming fear
That as she stood in the village shop,
Somebody might hear.

All through the winter nights and days
The ticking never ceased,
And when May came with leaves and flowers
The sound of it increased.

Miss Williams put on her grey straw hat
To deaden the awful tick
And went along the sunken lane
Where the buttercups grew thick.

They powdered her shoes with golden dust,
The grasses waved to her knee.
The sun shone on her guinea-gold –
Miss Williams did not see.

When she reached the end of the sunken lane
And came to the road beyond,
She crossed the road and opened the gate
That lead to the round field-pond.

Tick, tick, tick went the beetle
In poor Miss Williams' head;
As firmly she marched into the pond
And lay down as if in her bed.

The duck-weed covered her pale blue eyes,
Her hands were crossed on her breast;
The death-watch beetle flew back to the church
And Miss Williams was at rest.

Elizabeth Wills-Browne

Step 1

Questions

1 How real was the noise to Miss Williams?

2 What was her overwhelming fear? Why do we feel sorry for her?

Step 2

Statements

1 This is a poem about insanity.

2 Miss Williams cannot be at peace until she has put the noise out of her head.

Step 3

References

'The death-watch beetle from the church'

'And her pale blue eyes were haunted'

Step 4

Personal response

How strongly has the poet conveyed to you the torture that Miss Williams was undergoing? Write a newspaper report of the incident that in no way understands what was going on in Miss Williams' head.

The battery hen

Oh, I am a battery hen,
On me back there's not a germ,
I never scratched a farmyard,
And I never pecked a worm.
I never had the sunshine
To warm me feathers through.
Eggs I lay. Every day.
For the likes of you.

When you has them scrambled,
Piled up on your plate,
It's me what you should thank for that.
I never lays them late,
I always lays them reg'lar,
I always lays them right,
I never lays them brown,
I always lays them white.

But it's no life for a battery hen.
In me box I'm sat,
A funnel stuck out from the side,
My pellets comes down that.
I gets a squirt of water,
Every half a day,
Watchin' with me beady eye,
Me eggs roll away.

I lays them in a funnel,
Strategically placed
So that I don't kick 'em
And let them go to waste.
They rolls off down the tubing
And up the gangway quick,
Sometimes I gets to thinkin',
'That could have been a chick!'

I might have been a farmyard hen,
Scratchin' in the sun,
There might have been a crowd of chicks,
After me to run.
There might have been a cockerel fine
To pay us his respects,
Instead of sittin' here,
Till someone comes and wrings our necks.

I see the Time and Motion clock
Is saying nearly noon.
I 'spec me squirt of water
Will come flyin' at me soon,
And then me spray of pellets
Will nearly break me leg,
And I'll bite the wire nettin'
And lay one more bloody egg.

Pam Ayres

124

Step 1

Questions

1 What lines upset you most?

2 Why are chickens kept like this?

Step 2

Statements

1 Despite being a humorous poet, Pam Ayres obviously feels deeply about the plight of the battery hen.

2 The Oxfordshire dialect helps give the poem a country feel.

Step 3

References

'When you has them scrambled,'

'I might have been a farmyard hen,/Scratchin' in the sun,'

Step 4

Personal response

What farm animals do you think are cruelly treated?

Do you laugh at all at this poem? Compare this with 'Hunstman blow your bloody horn' (page 116).

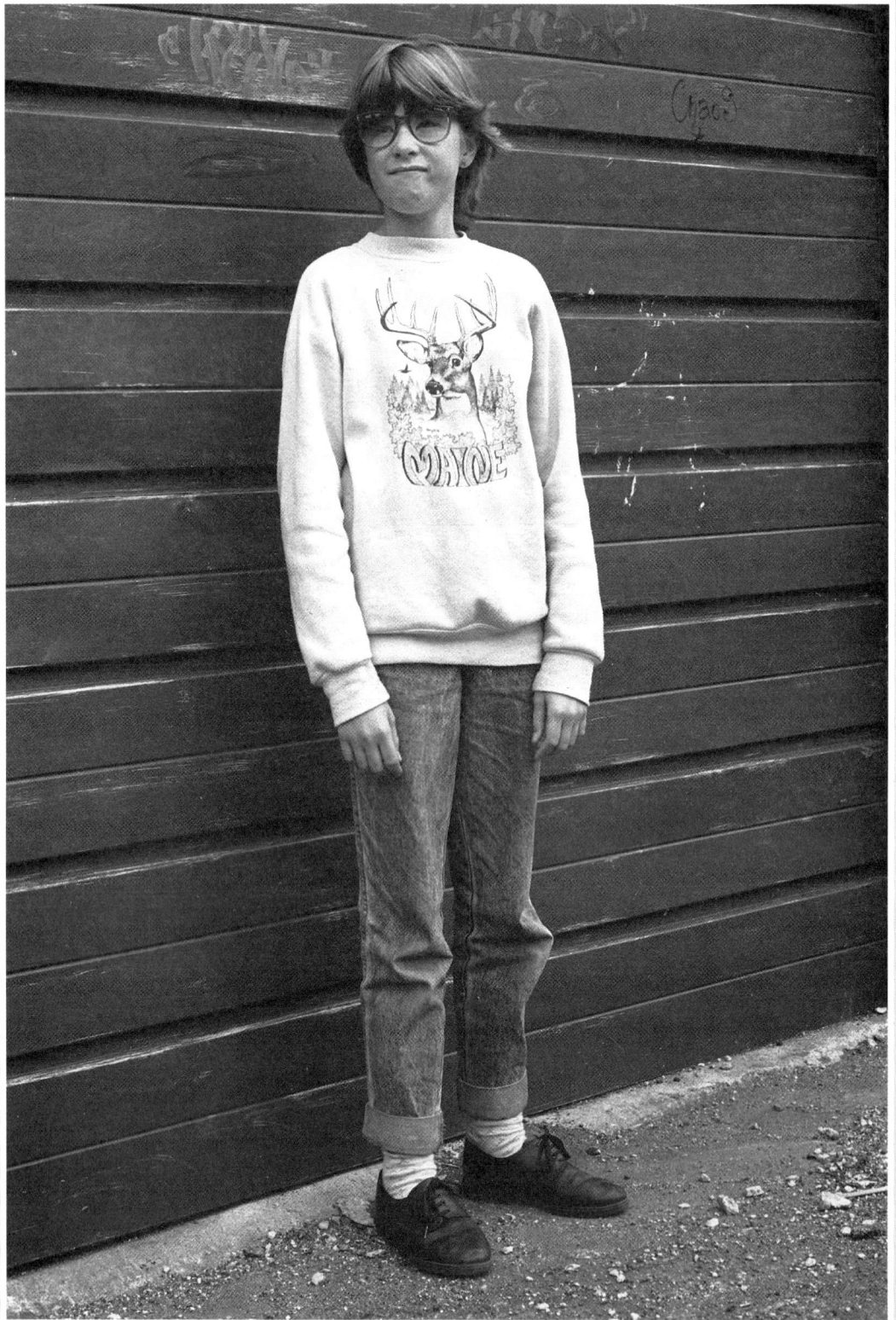

Tich Miller

Tich Miller wore glasses
with elastoplast-pink frames
and had one foot three sizes larger than the other.

When they picked two teams for outdoor games
she and I were always the last two
left standing by the wire-mesh fence.

We avoided one another's eyes,
stooping, perhaps, to re-tie a shoelace,
or affecting interest in the flight

of some fortunate bird, and pretended
not to hear the urgent conference:
'Have Tubby!' 'No, no, have Tich!'

Usually they chose me, the lesser dud,
and she lolloped, unselected,
to the back of the other team.

At eleven we went to different schools.
In time I learned to get my own back,
sneering at hockey-players who couldn't spell.

Tich died when she was twelve.

Wendy Cope

Step 1

Questions

1 What is the poem about?

2 What do you feel for (a) the poet, (b) Tich Miller?

Step 2

Statements

1 The poet has obviously experienced what she
wrote about.

2 She uses the words 'Tubby' and 'Tich' for a
purpose.

Step 3

References

'with elastoplast-pink frames'

'and she lolloped, unselected,/to the back of the
other team.'

Step 4

Personal response

In small groups, act out the part of the poem where
Tich and Tubby are the last to be picked for the
teams. Then write how you felt during the acting of
the scene.

M1 way of life

Bloody, battered, tattered thing
Which is body
Which is wing
What kind of bird
It's hard to say
As you lay squashed
On a motor way
But the marks in your blood
Are sharp and clear
A Dunlop 'safety' tyre
Has just been here.

Spike Milligan

Step 1

Questions

1 Why might Spike Milligan have written this poem?

2 Are the last two lines meant to be funny?

Step 2

Statements

1 You do not have to write a long poem to put across your feelings.

2 Man's love affair with the motor car has damaged nature in many ways.

Step 3

References

'Bloody, battered, tattered thing'

'A Dunlop 'safety' tyre/Has just been here.'

Step 4

Personal response

How does this poem compare with your own feelings on the subject?

Jock

He came each year, between leaf-fall and first hard frost,
He came at night to the unlocked barn of billowing hay.
One of the 'day men' would say, "Jock's back, Boss."
My father carried tea and bread and cheese,
And came back shaking his head, unusually quiet.

Each year, my grandmother asked him to our Christmas table.
And he would say in his posh voice,
"Thanking you all, but maybe next year."
He never did come, but stayed a dark shadow in the warm barn.

Every Lady Day, he was back on the road again,
Lazarus white, twitching and staggering on his way.
We watched him pass through the thickening hedgerows.
The 'day men' raked the hay, threw out the meths bottles,
Told my father he had gone and shook their heads.

And then, two years, three years passed,
"He'll not come now," they said.
But every year, my father left the barn unlocked,
And we watched the road until darkfall.
"See if you can find anything out," we begged.

My grandmother folded the socks and scarf
In tissue paper and slipped them into the drawer.
On my way to fetch the Christmas log, I looked in the barn
And saw my father and all his men standing, heads bared,
In a hard frost.

Marjorie Appleby

Step 1

Questions

1 When did Jock come every year to live in the barn and when did he leave?

2 When he went on his way again, why was he 'twitching and staggering'?

Step 2

Statements

1 Jock was a tramp who must once have been fairly well off but who had ruined his life through drink.

2 When he was dying, he returned to the barn which was 'home' to him.

Step 3

References

''Thanking you all but maybe next year.''

'He never did come'

'every year my father left the barn unlocked'

Step 4

Personal response

How can you tell from the poem that Jock and the farmer and his workers treated each other with friendliness and respect?

Write about a person you know and feel sorry for.

Harvest hymn

We spray the fields and scatter
    The poison on the ground
So that no wicked wild flowers
    Upon our farm be found.
We like whatever helps us
    To line our purse with pence;
The twenty-four-hour broiler-house
    And neat electric fence.

All concrete sheds around us
    And Jaguars in the yard,
The telly lounge and deep-freeze
    Are ours from working hard.

We fire the fields for harvest,
    The hedges swell the flame,
The oak trees and the cottages
    From which our fathers came.
We give no compensation,
    The earth is ours today,
And if we lose on arable,
    Then bungalows will pay.

All concrete sheds. . .etc.

John Betjeman

Step 1

Questions

1 What is the poet complaining about?

2 What are the similarities of this and 'The battery hen' (page 124)?

Step 2

Statements

1 This is written to a harvest hymn tune and verse.

2 This technique is called a parody.

Step 3

References

'So that no wicked wild flowers'

'And Jaguars in the yard,'

Step 4

Personal response

Write a reply from a farmer, saying how the poem gives a completely unfair view.

Crowd violence

I dreamed I was at Millwall;
The boys was all stood about:
It was half-time in the hooligan match
When suddenly football broke out.
I blame the parents myself;
I'd stick the boot in the Mother;
Those kids was kickin' a ball about
When they could have been kickin' each other.
But then a policeman on a white horse
Cleared the pitch, an arrested both teams.
Incidentally, Millwall was winnin'
Which just goes to prove it's a dream.

Les Barker

Step 1

Questions

1 Is this a suitable subject for poetry?

2 How do you know it is a dream?

Step 2

Statements

1 The poet's attitude to violence among football crowds is clear.

2 He could be a Millwall fan.

Step 3

References

'I'd stick the boot in the Mother;'

'When they could have been kicking each other.'

Step 4

Personal response

What is your attitude to violence in football crowds?

What odd thing have you dreamed about any sporting event or something sporting involving yourself?

Mountain lion

Climbing through the January snow, into the Lobo Canyon
Dark grow the spruce-trees, blue is the balsam, water sounds still unfrozen,
    and the trail is still evident.
Men!
Two men!
Men! The only animal in the world to fear!

They hesitate.
We hesitate.
They have a gun.
We have no gun.

Then we all advance, to meet.

Two Mexicans, strangers, emerging out of the dark and snow and inwardness
    of the Lobo Valley.
What are they doing here on this vanishing trail?

What is he carrying?
Something yellow.
A deer?

Qué tiene, amigo?
León –

He smiles, foolishly, as if he were caught doing wrong.
And we smile, foolishly, as if we didn't know.
He is quite gentle and dark-faced.

It is a mountain lion,
A long, long slim cat, yellow like a lioness.
Dead.

He trapped her this morning, he says, smiling foolishly.

Lift up her face,
Her round, bright face, bright as frost.
Her round, fine-fashioned head, with two dead ears;
And stripes in the brillant frost of her face, sharp, fine dark rays
Dark, keen, fine rays in the brilliant frost of her face.
Beautiful dead eyes.

Hermoso es!

They go out towards the open;
We go on into the gloom of Lobo.
And above the trees I found her lair,
A hole in the blood orange brilliant rocks that stick up, a little cave.
And bones, and twigs, and a perilous ascent.

So, she will never leap up that way again, with the yellow flash of a mountain
    lion's long shoot!
And her bright striped frost-face will never watch any more, out of the shadow
    of the cave in the blood-orange rock,
Above the trees of the Lobo dark valley-mouth!

Instead, I look out.
And out to the dim of the desert, like a dream, never real;
To the snow of the Sangre de Cristo mountains, the ice of the mountains of
    Picoris,
And near across at the opposite step of snow, green trees motionless standing
    in snow, like a Christmas toy.

And I think in this empty world there was room for me and a mountain lion.
And I think in the world beyond, how easily we might spare a million or two
    of humans
And never miss them.
Yet what a gap in the world, the missing white frost-face of that slim yellow
    mountain lion!

D.H. Lawrence

Step 1

Questions

1 What would be lost if the second verse were written:

'They hesitated and so did we.
They had a gun and we did not.'?

2 How is the author's use of variety in style and verse form throughout the poem shown clearly in the first verse?

Step 2

Statements

1 The author has a contempt for human beings.

2 In describing the beauty of the lion the author keeps reminding the reader that it is dead.

Step 3

References

'He is quite gentle...'

'smiles, foolishly' (repeated)

'...what a gap in the world.'

Step 4

Personal response

Write a comment on this response to the poem:
'OK, I agree that if there was only one mountain lion in that area, it's a pity to kill it. But the poet's not against hunting. All he's saying is that you shouldn't shoot rare and beautiful animals.'

Compare this poem with 'Huntsman blow your bloody horn' (page 116).

The priest speaks

I well remember, many years ago
during the War, one day I was at Lundë
when they were holding a recruiting board.
All men were talking of our country's hour
of danger – asking what the future held.
    There, seated at the table, in between
the Bailiff and the Sergeant, was the Captain;
each boy in turn he carefully examined
and then enrolled and took him for a soldier.
The room was packed, and from the green, outside,
we heard the laughter of the waiting lads . . .
    A name was called; another lad stepped up,
pale as the snow along the glacier's edge.
They called him nearer. He approached the table.
He had his right hand bandaged with a cloth.
He gasped and swallowed, fumbling after words
but finding none, despite the Captain's orders.
Then, in conclusion, with his cheeks on fire,
his tongue now faltering, now pouring words,
he mumbled something of a scythe that slipped
and sliced his finger off . . . A silence fell,
some exchanged glances, others pursed their lips,
their silent looks pelted the boy like stones;
and though his eyes were shut, he felt the blows.
At last the Captain rose, an old, grey man,
he spat, showed him the door, and said "Get out!"
    The boy went. Men fell back on either side
so that he ran the gauntlet through their ranks.
He reached the door, and then took to his heels.
Upwards he ran, up through the woods and moorland,
limping and staggering among the rocks
back to his home, high on the mountainside.

Henrik Ibsen

Step 1

Questions

1 What does the title add to your feeling about the poem?

2 How is the contrasting keenness of the other recruits stressed?

Step 2

Statements

1 The hostility to the boy is made to seem as vicious as a physical assault.

2 The poet makes no judgements.

Step 3

References

'pale as the snow'

'. . . his cheeks on fire,' (look for similar contrasts)

'. . . an old, grey man,'

Step 4

Personal response

Write a conversation between the boy and his mother when he returned to his house 'high on the mountainside'.

Step 5

Section assignments

1 Choose two poems about people and show how the poets have made you sympathetic towards them.

2 Write a review for a newspaper of the poems in this section, recommending some poems in particular to your readers.

General assignments

It will help you if you just browse through the book before starting on any of these assignments. Pick the poems you feel most personality involved with or the ones you have identified with strongly. You will write better if you do.

1 Look at the three Douglas Dunn poems (pages 26, 29 and 119). How are they alike? What things does he record that makes it seem like your street, _or_ how does he paint such a vivid picture of the street that you feel you are there? Write a poem about a street or road you know well.

2. Choose three poems about old people. What are their similarities? What words or phrases do the poets use in their descriptions of old age? Do you feel they are in sympathy with the problems of old age or just recording what they see? Write a poem about your grandma or grandad.

3. Pick two or three poems about the countryside and show how they differ from two or three poems about a town. Pick out phrases which you think are relevant to each. Then read 'Seasonal' by Anna Adams (page 38). How is she writing both about the country and the town? What are her feelings about the contrasting modes of life in each environment?

4 Pick three poems that you feel will be the most relevant in this anthology by the end of the century. Say why you have picked them. Then pick two poems you think have not much relevance to today or to young people. Say why you have picked them. What subject do you feel poets should be writing about today?

5 Pick some poems about childhood from the 'Do you remember?' section. How did the various childhoods compare with yours? Quote lines in the poems where you felt that your childhood was just like that. Write a poem about a particular incident in your childhood.

6 Choose three poems in which you think the poet is criticising modern life and its practices. Say precisely why the poet wants us to think deeply about the issue he or she has raised. Why is the Green Movement (Friends of the Earth and Greenpeace) so appealing to the young people of today? Write a poem about how we are treating the Earth.

7 Pick three poems in which you feel sorry for the person the poet is writing about. How does the poet get our sympathies for the person? What particular aspect of their lives does the poet show us? Write a poem about someone you feel sorry for.

8 Which five poems did you like best in this anthology? Say why they mean more to you than any of the others. What problems did you have in picking the top five? Quote any phrases or structures that particularly appealed to you.

9 Choose three funny poems. Quote some funny lines and say what is funny about them. Also say whether you think the poet had a serious purpose in writing the poem. Why is humour a good way of getting your thoughts or feelings across to an audience? Try writing a funny rhymed poem of your own.

10 'That's just how I feel.' One of the skills of the poet is to express thoughts and feelings we all have. Choosing up to six of the poems and using quotes, say how your own feelings match those of the poets. Say why they do, if you can. Write a poem about the thing you feel most deeply about.

11 Choose three poems about odd or unusual people. How does the poet describe them? What should our attitude be to people who we do not regard as 'normal' either mentally or physically? Write a poem about a mentally-handicapped person or about someone with a physical disability.

12 Pick out three poems about cruelty. What are the poets writing about? How deeply do they feel about the subject they have chosen? Which poem is the most effective and why? Write your own poem about something you regard as a cruel act.

13 Pick out three poems about death. Why is death a common subject for poetry? Why might a few verses of poetry be more effective than a long prose piece about the subject? How have the three poets tackled the subject? Which poem did you find most effective? Write your own poem about death.

14 Learn a poem by heart. Practise it at home as if you were an actor. Think of the stresses and intonations you will use. Your main job is to get the feeling or the message across to an audience. Most people speak too quickly. Recite the poem to the class, slowly and with feeling.

15 If you cannot bear to face an audience, write down instructions for how a poem should be read. Copy out the poem and put notes and instructions on it for the reader.

Acknowledgements

We are grateful to the following for permission to reproduce photographs:
Anne Bolt, page 65; Colorsport, page 117; Hulton Deutsch Collection, pages 31, 33, 40–41; Ingrid Gavshon/Photo Co-op, pages 97, 110–111; Camilla Jessel, pages 72, 73; Network, pages 7 & 19 (photo: Mike Abrahams); Oxford Scientific Films, pages 53 & 60 (photo: Jack Dermid); Brian Shuel, pages 36, 48–49, 88; Janine Wiedel, pages 54–55, 98–99.

Commissioned photographs: John Birdsall, pages 75, 94, 126 (posed by model): Graham Portlock of Pentaprism, pages 8–9, 81, 104–5, 113, 128, 132–3; Bruce Rae, pages 14–15, 26–7, 44–5, 120.

We are grateful to the following for permission to reproduce copyright material:

the author's agents for the poems 'Stereotype' and 'Finders Keepers' by John Agard: W H Allen & Co Plc for the poem 'Dumb Insolence' by Adrian Mitchell; the author, Majorie Appleby for her poem 'Jock' from *Yorkshire Poets* (1982); the author, Les Barker for his poems 'Huntsman blow your bloody horn' and 'Crowd violence' (c) Mrs Ackroyd Enterprises; the author, Alan Barrett for his poems 'Grandma's Funeral' and 'Betrayal'; The Bodley Head Ltd, on behalf of the author for the poem 'At Any Rate' by James Michie; the author, Martin Booth for his poem 'Following Cows through the Village of Ash', Copyright Martin Booth 1985; the author, Keith Bosley for his poem 'Number 14' from *Stations* (Anvil Press Poetry, 1979) (c) Keith Bosley; the author, Elizabeth Wills Browne for her poem 'Miss Williams and the Death-Watch Beetle' from *Sotheby's International Poetry Competition 1982 Anthology* pub Arvon Foundation); Jonathan Cape Ltd, on behalf of the author's Estate for the poem 'Mrs Middleditch' from *Collected Poems* by William Plomer; the author's agents for the poem 'By St Thomas Water' from *Collected Poems* by Charles Causley (J M Dent & Sons Ltd); Chatto & Windus Ltd for the poem 'Sea Coal' by Pippa Little from *New Chatto Poets*; the author, Cal Cothier for his poem 'What goes into Chicken Pies'; the author, Stewart Conn for his poem 'Ferret' from *In the Kibble Palace* (pub Bloodaxe Books, 1987); the author, Jan Dean for her poem 'Writing' from *Kingfisher Book of Children's Poetry* edited by M Rosen; Andre Deutsch Ltd for the poem 'Daniel Lambert'

142

from *Poems* by Phillip Oakes; Dolphin Concert Productions Ltd for the poems 'Oh I Wish I'd Looked After Me Teeth' and 'The Battery Hen' by Pam Ayres, Copyright Pam Ayres; Faber & Faber Ltd for the poems 'Reading Scheme' and 'Tich Miller' from *Making Cocoa for Kingsley Amis* by Wendy Cope, 'The Patricians' and 'A Removal from Terry Street' by Douglas Dunn, 'Ballad of the Two Left Hands' from *Barbarians* by Douglas Dunn, 'Baby Song' from *Jack Straw's Castle* by Thom Gunn, 'The Early Purges' from *Death Of A Naturalist* by Seamus Heaney, 'Touched with Fire' from *The Whitsun Weddings* by Philip Larkin, 'Warty Bliggins the toad' from *Archie And Mehitabel* by Don Marquis, 'The Dare' from *Midnight Forest and Other Poems* by Judith Nicholls, 'Arthur' from *A State of Justice* by Tom Paulin; the author's agents for the poem 'The Skip' from *The Memory of War and Children in Exile* by James Fenton (Salamander Press and Penguin Books); the author, Gregory Harrison for his poem 'Distracted the Mother said to her Boy' from *A Fourth Poetry Book* (Oxford University Press) (c) Gregory Harrison; the author's agents for the poem 'Long Distance' from *Tony Harrison Selected Poems* by Tony Harrison (Penguin, 1987); the author, Barry Heath for his poem 'Guy Fawkes'; The Hogarth Press Ltd, the translator and the author's estate for the poem 'Candles' by C P Cavafy from *Complete Poems* translated by Rae Dalven; The Hogarth Press Ltd and the author for the poem 'The Old Women' from *The Drowning Wave* by George Mackay Brown; the author, Brian Jones and Alan Ross Ltd for the poem 'Visiting Miss Emily' from *Poems* by Brian Jones (Alan Ross Ltd, 1966) (c) London Magazine; the author, Even Jones for his poem 'The Song of the Banana Man'; James McGibbon, the executor of the author's estate, for the poems 'Emily writes such a good letter' and 'The Engine Drain' by Stevie Smith from *The Collected Poems of Stevie Smith* (Penguin Modern Classics); the author's agent, for the poem 'Teevee' from *Jamboree Rhymes for All Times* by Eve Merriam. Copyright (c) 1962, 1964, 1966, 1973, 1984, by Merriam. All rights reserved; Spike Milligan Productions Ltd for the poem 'M1 Way of Life' from *Open Heart University* by Spike Milligan (Penguin 1980); John Murray (Publishers) Ltd for the poem 'Harvest Hymn' by John Betjeman from *Collected Poems*; Oxford University Press for the poem 'The Trap' from *The Apple Barrel* by Jon Stallworthy (1974); The New Yorker for the poem 'The O-Filler' by Alistair Reid (c) Alistair Reid; the author's estate for the poem 'Suddenly Walking Along the Open Road' by Mervyn Peake; Penguin Books Ltd for the poem 'Hugger Mugger' from *Hot Dog and Other Poems* by Kit Wright (Kestrel Books, 1981), copyright (c) 1981 Kit Wright; Rivelin Grapheme Press for the poems 'Seasonal' and 'Another of Those Boring Bomb Stories' by Anna Adams (c) Anna Adams, first published *Purple and Green* (Rivelin Grapheme Press 1985); the author, Vernon Scannell for his poem 'Uncle Edward's Affliction'; Virago Press Ltd for the poem 'The Fat Black Woman Goes Shopping' from *The Fat Black Woman's Poems* by Grace Nichols, Copyright (c) Grace Nichols 1984 (Virago Press Ltd, 1984); George Weidenfield & Nicholson Ltd for the poem 'When I was a Kid' from *I Never Saw My Father Nude* by Dan Coleman.

We have been unable to trace the copyright holders in the following and would appreciate any information that would enable us to do so;

the poem 'Dead Men's Shirts' by Stewart Brown from *The Gregory Awards* (Martin Secker & Warburg); the poem 'The Diet' by Maureen Burge from *In the Pink* (Women's Press Ltd); the poem 'Home' by William Cooke in *Outposts 115*, Winter 1977; the poem 'Janet Waking' by John Crowe Ransom from *Sounds and Silences* (Dell Publishing Co); the poem 'Our Greenhouse' from *In Membership of My Days* by Richard Harris (Michael Joseph Ltd 1975); the poem 'Stopping Places' by Molly Holden from *Poetry Dimension Annual 5* edited by Danny Abse (Robson books, 1978); the poem 'The Old Couple' by F Pratt Green from *Poetry Dimension Annual 5* edited by Danny Abse (Robson Books 1978); the poem 'The Butcher' by Hugo Williams from *Penguin Book of Contemporary Poetry* (1982).

Cover: *Crazy Talk* by Andrzej Dudzinski. Source: Oxford Scientific Films, Oxford.

Designed by Jenny Portlock of Pentaprism

The other Steps books

Steps to GCSE Success   0 582 20676 6
Steps to GCSE Literature   0 582 01457 3

Steps: a basic English course
        Book 1   0 582 20145 4
             2   0 582 20146 2
             3   0 582 20147 0
             4   0 582 20148 9

Longman Group UK Limited
*Longman House. Burnt Mill. Harlow. Essex. CM20 2JE. England
and Associated Companies throughout the World.*

© Longman Group UK Limited 1989

First published 1989
ISBN 0 582 03059 5

*Set in Linotron 202 on 11/13pt Souvenir
Produced by Longman Group (FE) Ltd
Printed in Hong Kong*